Living Among Sasquatch: a Primer

by Dave Gibson

foreword by Richard H. Nilsen

ISBN #: 978-1-329-77406-3

This book is dedicated to my loving wife, research partner, and one terrific 'Squatcher, Pamela, without whom this book would not have been written.

To all of my Sasquatch Facebook friends who guided me along my learning path of all things Sasquatch.

To authors Jeff Meldrum, Steve Kulls, Loren Coleman, John Green, Grover Krantz, and all of the other authors who shared their experiences and knowledge in books.

To all of you amateur field researchers, our boots on the ground, seeking answers to which we're not sure of the questions.

And to our local Sasquatch, especially Pamela's special young hairy friend, who befriended us and didn't kill us.

Table of Contents:

Foreword.. 6

Introduction.. 8

Chapter 1: the Beginning... 11

Chapter 2: Bear.. 14

Chapter 3: Felling the Tree.. 18

Chapter 4: Odd Animal Noises................................... 24

Chapter 5: Snow! And Good Neighbors..................... 26

Chapter 6: Toboggans.. 29

Chapter 7: Return From Florida................................. 31

Chapter 8: Our First Footprint................................... 32

Chapter 9: Shaking Tree.. 36

Chapter 10: the Hand Print.. 38

Chapter 11: Again With The Well.............................. 46

Chapter 12: Researching Bigfoot............................... 48

Chapter 13: More Footprints...................................... 50

Chapter 14: Footprints and a Baggie.......................... 54

Chapter 15: Sasquatch's House.................................. 58

Chapter 16. The Hand Print   67

Chapter 17: The Research Continued in Florida.......... 72

Chapter 18: Pamela's Sasquatch Dream..................... 75

Chapter 19: Sasquatches in South Carolina................ 77

Chapter 20: Sasquatches in Virginia.......................... 80

Chapter 21: Gifting.. 81

Chapter 22: Game Cameras.. 82

Chapter 23: Hit by a Tree.. 83

Chapter 24: File Under "C".. 85

Chapter 25: Sasquatch Signs...................................... 87

Chapter 26: Favorite Stories...................................... 90

Chapter 27: Where Are The Bodies............................ 93

Chapter 28: the Minnesota Iceman............................. 95

Chapter 29: the Iroquois Stone Giants....................... 98

Chapter 30: Back in the Adirondacks......................... 94

Chapter 31: Holy Effin' Crap..................................... 104

Chapter 32: Sasquatch Groups................................... 108

Chapter 33: Another Hand Print................................. 111

Chapter 34: Odd Happenings...................................... 112

Chapter 35: the Professionals Come In....................... 115

Chapter 36: Gone 'Squatchin'.. 117
Chapter 37: Another Print.. 125
Chapter 38: the Washers... 127
Chapter 39: Sasquatch Chatter... 129
Chapter 40: Sasquatch Poop?.. 130
Chapter 41: the Professionals Step Back In........................... 133
Chapter 42: the Horse's Mane.. 134
Chapter 43: the Smell!... 136
Chapter 44: the Gifting Stump.. 137
Chapter 45: Eye Shine and Lights.. 140
Chapter 46: Infrasound.. 144
Chapter 47: the Steak.. 145
Chapter 48: Sasquatch Easter Eggs....................................... 146
Chapter 49: Sasquatch Intelligence.. 151
Chapter 50: The Real Wayne's World.................................... 152
Chapter 51: Pamela's Sasquatch Friend................................. 153
Chapter 52: More From the Gifting Stump............................. 155
Chapter 53: Searching for Sasquatch..................................... 158
Chapter 54: Humm.. 159
Chapter 55: Signature Markers.. 160
Chapter 56: Footprint.. 164
Chapter 57: Whoops.. 165
Chapter 58: Stench in the Morning.. 166
Chapter 59: Sasquatch and the Neighbors.............................. 167
Chapter 60: Chinese Symbols Continued............................... 168
Chapter 61: the End.. 169

Foreword

A pastor friend of mine used to say, "A man with a theory is always at the mercy of a man with an experience."

For Dave Gibson, a man I've known more than two decades, his theories radically changed with the encounters he experienced in the Adirondack Park between 2013 and 2015.

Dave's past has been as a businessman, computer programmer, entrepreneur and community minded promoter of live music, literature, boating and the local Boys and Girls Club. If his past contains any U.F.O./ alien abduction scenarios, paranormal activities or séances, it's news to me.

As the pages of this book will show, Dave backed into Sasquatch investigations unwillingly and with great skepticism. And while the observer can find as many opinions about the existence of and activities of Bigfoot as there are people you talk to, Dave's humor, lack of hyperbole and resistance to make any bald-faced claims are both refreshing and laudable.

But better than all that, this book is a good read. His conversational style, lack of long, drawn out scientific reports or reliance on supposed authorities leaves the reader with the option of shrugging off another man's observations or an acceptance of what is difficult to dispute without resorting to even wilder theories.

This writer is one of those who find a guided creation story easier to believe than random evolutionary theory. In other words, Sasquatch could as well be a part of a divine being's plan as anything else. I, for one, like to think God has a sense of humor. Why else the duck-billed platypus? (Another mammal long thought to be myth.) But I also concede the impossibility of proving my beliefs.

I would say this is Dave's viewpoint. The occurrences cataloged herein are enough to convince him and if they don't convince the reader, no big deal.

It's a good read regardless as well as an intriguing mystery. Like Dave, I tend to enjoy mysteries that may never be totally solved. It's the voyage more than the arrival.

-- Richard H. Nilsen, M.F.A. author "Trying to Help People: Fifty Years in the Wilderness" and "An Old-Fashioned Shooting," Adirondack Park, Dec. 2015.

Introduction:

Everything in this book that happened to my wife and me is true. The details and conversations are as I can best recall and written honestly.

I write a blog and regularly record events of any significance, so it has acted as a diary. Blog entries are written in the evening of the day I wrote about, or the morning after. This blog is about our life in our tiny town on a mountain in the southern foothills of the Adirondack Mountains of upstate New York and is mainly about us buying ten acres of wooded land, clearing part of it, and working towards building a small off grid home. Much to my surprise, the blog is also sprinkled with entries of Sasquatch.

I'm starting off the book without much mention of Sasquatch. I want you to get a flavor of where we're living and what we're doing. The Adirondack Park is the largest in the lower 48 states at 6.1 million acres, of which 2.3 million acres is protected state owned forest preserve, overseen by the Adirondack Park Agency. The state owned land is "forever wild" and the privately held land is regulated. In my area, for example, the minimum lot size to build a home on is 8 acres. Regulations vary by region. If you look down at the park from space (you can do so with Google Earth) you will see almost nothing but trees, lakes, ponds, and rivers, with small towns scattered about.

My own town has 38,000 acres and a mere 550 people. There is plenty of room for a creature who didn't want to be seen to conceal itself.

By the way, this book is for everyone. For those of you experienced 'Squatchers, please pardon the explanation of basic Sasquatch terms and definitions for the benefit of those readers new to the subject.

Whitehall, New York has become somewhat famous for it's Sasquatch sightings. Perhaps the most notable report was by a Whitehall police officer and a State Trooper who both saw a Sasquatch in 1976. There is so much Sasquatch activity there (called a "hot spot") it attracts many paranormal TV shows. The show *Finding Bigfoot* was there recently to film another episode. My town is 52 miles as the crow flies from there.

Things that make you go hmmmmm.... The word "Adirondack" comes from the Native American Mohawk *ratirontaks*. It means "they eat trees". It has been said that the Algonquins got through the Adirondack's brutal winter by eating tree bark. Consider, though that Native Americans consider Sasquatch to be the "forest people", another tribe of Native Americans, not apes. Could the Iroquois have been referring to Sasquatch and not Algonquins?

You'll probably notice that I won't mention the name of my town. I don't want uninvited people coming around, especially with guns, to spook off our family of Sasquatch or worse yet shoot one. I'm only a tad bit uneasy living with them, since they're so large and powerful. They could do me in quickly if they so choose. But, so far anyway, they haven't chosen to do that. But if you're a serious researcher, I'm sure you can track me down, and if you do, I'd be happy to chat with you about it, or even show you around, one or two of you at a time.

Enjoy the book. If the topic of Sasquatch is new to you, or if you're a skeptic, I understand. So was I until the late summer of 2014. I hope, like me, you'll learn to recognize the signs of Sasquatch. Maybe you're living with them too, and just haven't noticed yet, because you didn't know what to look for. After reading this, perhaps you will.

Just a note too about the odd arrangement of "chapters". Much of this book was lifted from my blog, an online diary of sorts. Some chapters are lengthy, some are only a few sentences. I certainly could have combined many short chapters into longer ones, or grouped them by subject, but I chose not to for several reasons. First, you will understand our experiences better since you can follow our encounters as they happened. Secondly, the dates may (or may not) have some relevance to things as they occurred. Since it is better to be safe than sorry, I left the chapters as is

Dave Gibson
April 21, 2015

Chapter 1: the Beginning

My wife, Pamela, and I lived aboard our trawler for several years, cruising down the eastern seaboard and playing "we could live here!"

 But when we returned to upstate New York in the summer of 2012, we fell in love with the Adirondack Mountains all over again. I started looking around at property and houses online thinking that perhaps we could move back. When I mentioned this to my father-in-law, Earl, he said I should just buy the ten acres of land next to his property.

"I sold it to Ed. We put in a driveway. Ed stuck a trailer on it, intending to live there. Then Ed got sick and couldn't come up anymore from Pennsylvania. He should give you the family discount, because I gave him one when he bought it."

And so we did.

I hired a logging company to clear a few acres of it, which they did in the winter of 2012 and 2013. I made a cool $700 on the timber.

While we were going through the process of hiring an architect to design our house and getting something built, we needed someplace to live. Earl to the rescue again. He knew of a small cabin for rent just a mile from our property. We rented it sight unseen. How bad can it be? Heck, we'd been living on a 46' trawler for a few years with a few good sized dogs and a couple of cats.

"Are you sure you don't want to look at it first?" said Toni.

"Naw. We'll be fine," I replied, as I naively figured we'd have a place built in no time.

We arrived at the cabin in the spring of 2013. I was towing a U-Haul packed with things from the boat, which was on the hard and listed for sale. Earl told me right where the driveway to it was.

"Just past the white house on the corner is a guard rail. The driveway is right next to the guard rail." Well, we were there. We looked just past the guardrail and saw no driveway. Pam called her mom.

"We don't see a driveway," she said.

"Its there," said Judi.

We got out of the car and looked. There was something somewhat resembling a rutted dirt driveway that went down a steep hill. We couldn't see a cabin. We drove to Earl and Judi's house just down the road, pulled into their driveway and parked the car and U-Haul. We explained to Earl and Judi that we must have been in the wrong place.

"No, that's it," said Earl. Earl offered to tow the U-Haul there with his truck, which he did. He got to the guard rail and drove off the highway and down it. So did I. It was a leap of faith driving down there.

We arrived at the cabin, which was barely visible. Jim and Toni bought the cabin and 29 acres many years before, but haven't been there in a few years. Scrub pines had grown up all around it, hiding the cabin. Earl had a key and unlocked the door. We went inside. Maybe we should have looked at it first.

It is a saltbox design with a wall of windows facing south. On the first floor is a small kitchen, an eating area, a living room, and a bathroom. Upstairs are two small bedrooms. The little cabin felt roomy after our boat, but it was a mess. Dusty, messy, and covered in mouse poop everywhere. Our two cats were very excited, and spent the next few months eating very well.

Chapter 2: Bear

Over the next couple of weeks, I cleared out many of the scrub pines around the cabin. I used a hand saw, and finally a chain saw to do it. I wanted the trees to the south cleared out in particular. I could only clear about 75 feet before the land dropped off to a stream. This opened the cabin up a bit. Pam cheerfully hung up a few bird feeders filled with sunflower seeds, and we soon had many birds coming by

June 7, 2013. It was almost dark. All of a sudden, our dogs went nuts. They were at the windows barking like crazy. Pam and I ran over to see. It was a large black bear. It was apparently surprised to see someone living in the cabin, but at the same time it was very pleased to see the sunflower seeds in the bird feeders that Pam put out.

The bear sat down. It looked at us, meaning Pam and I and our three dogs, and then the bird feeders. Us... bird feeders. Us.... bird feeders.

Then it slowly got up, ambled over to the bird feeders, sat down, pulled the tops off, and downed them. All the while it was nonchalantly chowing down, our dogs were going ballistic. I was thankful to have the protection of a pane of glass between us and the bear 20 feet away. And then he ambled off, over the bank and down to the stream, and he was gone.

I don't recall exactly when this next episode happened, but it was a hot night that summer. The upstairs bedroom was stifling hot, so Pam decided to sleep on the couch downstairs. Shortly thereafter she came running back upstairs.

"Something very big walked past the cabin windows!!", she clamored.

"Probably the bear", I said.

"No! It was big! I'm not sleeping down there ever again!"

"The boogeyman?" I joked.

"I don't know, but it was big!"

OK then.

So life proceeded, and we began work on our own property. I hired a guy with a bulldozer and his son with an excavator to bulldoze all the stumps the loggers left and to smooth everything out on the land. It was amazing to me how quickly they worked.

The father, driving the bulldozer, was good, pushing stumps and rocks off to the side. But his son was amazing in the excavator, picking up stumps and rocks and easily tossing them. My guess his skill was derived from a lot of time at computer games.

I bought a tractor that year too, an old 1952 Ferguson TO-30. I used that to smooth off the land, and to cart rocks around. Lots and lots of rocks. Rocks. What to do with them? I started building stone walls. I piled them up in places for future rock gardens.

And then there was firewood to cut. I asked the loggers to leave me some logs so they could season for a year before cutting them up, which they did. I cut all I thought I needed, but next I decided I had to fell some trees for 2014's winter. It is best to cut trees a year before you'll burn them so they can season. It was a decision I would regret.

Chapter 3: Felling the Tree

I've cut down many trees in my day. So many, I couldn't hazard a guess. Still, I'm very careful about how I do it.

August 27, 2013. Pam had the Kia, so I took her little five speed Miata to our property. Today, I'm cutting trees, I declare to myself. I've had enough of rocks. I fetched my chainsaw from our storage trailer and headed down the hill.

I found a good sized tree, I looked around, checked to make sure the footing was good, and that I had an escape path. I notched it in the direction I wanted it to fall and back cut it so it was barely standing. I turned off the saw and set it down to the side. I easily pushed it, and as it started to fall, I stepped back in case it kicked. It fell with a resounding WHOMP!! I woke up sometime later laying on the ground.

I was paralyzed. I could blink and breathe, but I couldn't move. What happened? After a few minutes, I started to regain some feeling in my arms and legs. Laying next to me was a large sapling, maybe 20 or 25 feet long, a couple of inches in diameter where it smacked me square on the noggin. I slowly got up as I gradually regained feeling in my legs and left arm. Man, did my neck hurt. I slowly staggered up the hill to our deck's screen house. I sat down. I had no feeling at all in my right arm. There was no way I could drive to the hospital. I couldn't shift the Miata. Besides, I had no health insurance. It was canceled when I turned 60 years old.

Thankfully, I had a small cooler of beer, so I sat and waited. And drank beer. At least was a beautiful, sunny day. I'd enjoy it more if my neck didn't hurt so much, and if I could move my arm. How did this happen? There must have been a leaner that I didn't notice off to my left, and the reverberation of the tree shook it loose. How did it manage to hit me square on the head? Luck o' the Irish, I guess.

After a few hours, some feeling came back in my right arm. I hopped in Pam's Miata and slowly drove the mile back to our cabin. I went inside and sat on the couch. I thought about taking a shower. Maybe that would help. But then Pam came home.

"What's wrong?" she asked. Obviously I wasn't going to get away with this one, so I fessed up.

"I had an accident," I said.

"An accident? What happened?"

"I got hit on the head with a tree."

"Your going to the hospital. Right now."

"I can't. We don't have any insurance."

"No. You're going."

"Let's wait until morning," I replied. "Maybe I'll feel better in the morning."

"No. Get in the car."

"Nope. No way, no how." I can be a stubborn old cuss. There was no way I was going to the hospital. I put my foot down.

So we're headed for the hospital, and I said to Pam "Take me to St. Mary's in Amsterdam. I don't like Nathan Littauer for stuff like this."

We arrived at St. Mary's emergency room. I don't recall now all that went on, but after x-rays the doctor came to see us.

"You broke your neck," said the doc.

"So I should take it easy then?" said I.

"I'm transferring you to Albany Medical Center. We can't deal with an injury like this here."

Poor Pam could hardly keep her eyes open. She had gotten up early that day to drive her mother to St. Mary's for a foot operation. She was exhausted physically, and emotionally drained. I told her to go home. There was nothing she could do now. I was getting an ambulance ride to Albany Med and there would be a lot of sitting around and waiting. I could see that she was reluctant to let me go alone, but she needed sleep. It was 10 PM.

"Just go," I said. "Go home and get some sleep. You can come when you wake up."

So shortly thereafter, I'm in an ambulance headed for Albany. This part is fuzzy. I wonder if they gave me pain meds? Anyway, I remember the emergency room being very busy, and a lot of uniformed police officers there. The next thing I remember, I was in a ward with a lot of other guys, presumably all with broken necks from falling trees. I don't know how many tests I had, but I remember that I had a lot of doctors visit.

Pam arrived at Albany Med at 4 AM. I was glad to see her, but that's not getting much sleep since the cabin is about an hour and a half from Albany.

X-rays showed two fractured vertebrae in my neck, C6 and C7. The fracture in C6 was next to a blood vessel that runs to my supposed brain. The docs didn't tell me what that meant, but the look on the doctors' faces were grim enough to tell me it was serious. And I saw a lot of docs. Trauma docs, spine specialists, dermatologists, podiatrists, I saw them all.

"What happened?" asked a grim faced doctor.

I tried to be flippant, as is my nature whenever I'm hit by a tree. "I was attacked by a tree. It hit me square on the head."

"A tree branch?"

"No. A tree. I cut a tree down, and another snuck up on me and whacked me for it."

They asked me many questions about how I felt. They were amazed when I told them that I didn't have a headache most of all, it seemed.

"No headache?"

"Nope. Not a thing. I hit my head on stuff all the time."

They shined a light into my eyeballs. "Follow my finger. You don't have a headache???" they all asked.

Nope.

I was about to ask one if he wanted me to pull his finger, but then I thought that I had better watch what I say. There's a mental ward here, for sure.

While I didn't think this was all that of big a deal, they admitted me.

While I was undergoing tests, I sent Pam home again for much needed rest. She was beat. She didn't want to go, and I could see tears welling up in her eyes, a combination of exhaustion and stress. But I convinced her and she left.

Pam took this photo below the next morning.

You can see the tree I cut pointed at ten o'clock and the sapling laying across it that came from the left. I never saw it coming. It was, I think, hung up in another tree and sprung from the vibrations of the crash of the big one I cut. It never made it all the way to the ground. Good thing. I might have been paralyzed, or killed. It's not that big around, but long, and it must have sprung like a whip.

After many hours in the ER waiting for a bed, I was taken to C5 which specializes in spine trauma. I think C5 is some kind of inside spinal injury joke, but I can't say enough good things about Albany Med and C5. The staff there is incredibly attentive and even politely laughed at my lame jokes. If you ever get hit by a tree, go to Albany Medical Center in Albany New York and ask for C5. I don't care where you live. You go to Albany Med and ask for C5. Tell them the Mountain Idiot sent you.

I spent three days at Albany Med. $45,000 if you're wondering.

Chapter 4: Odd Animal Noises

My accident happened in August of 2013, and it was now
October. I couldn't work on the property. I could go over and
drink beer with Pam and my in-laws, which we did regularly late
in the afternoon.   My mornings were spent saving the world on
Facebook with my astute political observations and witty
comments. My afternoons were usually spent watching old
westerns bought at the $5 bin at Walmart.   We don't have regular
TV. We stopped watching when we started cruising on Drift
Away, our old trawler, and we found we really didn't miss it.

It was a chilly morning on October 12, 2013. I had a fire in the
wood stove, our only source of heat. I was really starting to hate
this stupid neck brace I had to wear.   Olivia, our German
Shorthaired Pointer, was outside barking, and barking, and
barking.   Finally I got up and walked outside and yelled at her.
She ignored me. She was sitting at the edge of the woods, staring
intently in one direction. Then I heard it. Some odd animal
noise. Coyote? No. Owl? No. What is that?

I ran back inside and grabbed my Nikon. I didn't take the time to
take off the 300 mm zoom lens. I put it in auto mode, and ran
back outside.   The critter was still there. I put it in video mode
and held it as steady as I could.

The first couple of vocalizations were a cross between a yap and a
whoop. Then it changed to a kind of barking laugh. Olivia was
still barking.   Where were my two pit bulls, Chevy and Ruby?
Our dogs are a pack, and when one barks, they all bark, like
when we had the bear outside our windows.   When one charges
into the forest, they all charge.

I filmed it for a few minutes, figured I had enough for someone
to figure out what it was, and went back inside. Olivia insisted on
staying outside.   Fine.

When I walked into the cabin, Chevy (the tough male) was cowering on the couch. Ruby was hiding under a table. What the heck? They fear nothing.

I downloaded the video and watched it. The sound was pretty clear, good enough for someone to identify it. I uploaded it to You Tube using Movie Maker and posted a link to it on You Tube (if you enter this URL carefully in your browser, you can listen – https://www.youtube.com/watch?v=69IuQ4-rAec, or search on "sasquatch vocalization dave gibson"). The responses that came back were all over the place. Coyote, Fox, and even an owl. I googled all over Al Gore's internets and listened to everything I could find. The closest match was coyote, which we have in our area, but it didn't sound right. It was different.

Back on Facebook, I put my wit to work and joked that maybe it was Bigfoot. I got laughed at by my so called "friends".

I found and played all sorts of vocalizations by coyotes, foxes, owls, turkeys... nothing matched. I also got no reaction from my dogs. Just for kicks, I googled Sasquatch vocalizations and got an immediate reaction from Olivia and Chevy. Ruby hid under the table again.

A short time later, bored in the cabin and wearing a neck brace that didn't fit right, I googled Bigfoot. I found some research sites, but nothing too interesting. I tried Sasquatch and found a few sites that didn't look too crazy. On a lark, I sent a link to my You Tube video to a Sasquatch research group in the Pacific Northwest and one in Ontario. Pacific Northwest said it sounded something like their Sasquatch but a different dialect. Dialect? As in language? Nonsense.

Ontario came back and said it was definitely a juvenile Sasquatch. Yep OK. Whatever.

25

Chapter 5: Snow! And Good Neighbors

It snows in upstate New York. I know that. But holy crap, did it snow. I think it snowed everyday, at least a half inch to an inch. And then, of course, there were the snowstorms.

It was December 17, 2013. We had at least a couple of feet of snow on the ground. We didn't plow our driveway because our Kia Sorento is all-wheel drive, which we can lock it in four wheel drive. We just drove in and out. But Pam was headed out our driveway, which is narrow, long, and steep, with a hill on one side and a drop off to a creek on the other.

"I'm stuck," she said as she stomped back into the cabin.

So I went out to unstick it, and made it worse. It was in snow, of course, but under that was ice. I was sliding sideways into the creek.

I went inside and called AAA. They sent out a tow truck which arrived in a short time.

"I can't get you out of there!" said the driver.

"Why not?" I asked.

"You're down there a couple of hundred feet! My cable ain't that long." and off he went.

Now what? We live in the middle of nowhere. The Miata is in storage and the Kia is stuck. We planned on heading to Florida after the holidays in an old RV I bought from my brother-in-law, but we needed the Kia to tow Pam's horse. Pam turned to Facebook and put out a plea for help. It was answered within minutes. A friend of Pam's saw the message. She works for the guy that owns the hunting camp between our cabin and our property. He manages a gravel pit, and has a big four wheel drive truck with a plow and sander. He was there in no time. He introduced himself, and then surveyed the situation. I wasn't expecting much, but he said he could get me out.

First, he plowed his way down the driveway a bit, and then backed out of the driveway, turned around, and sanded where he plowed. He did this several times until he got within about 50 feet of the car. Then Brian pulled a towing strap out of his truck, attached it, and then crawled under the Kia and fastened to it. Pam got in the car, and as soon as Brian started pulling the Kia, Pam hit the gas and followed him right up the driveway.

"Thanks Brian! You saved our butts!" I happily exclaimed.

"No problem."

"How much do we owe you?"

Brian just looked at me and smiled, and said "Where are you

27

going to park now?"

"Probably on the landing on the road."

And then Brian plowed that out too.

"How much, Brian?   I need to pay you for you time and trouble."

And with that, Brian got in his truck and drove off.

Pam's Facebook friend said that Brian likes Bud Lite, so we bought him a case of that and brought it to the gravel pit. And up until we left for Florida in January, every time it snowed, Brian plowed our landing.

Chapter 6: Toboggans

For the next few weeks, we hiked up and down our driveway to get to our car on the landing by the road. I bought a couple of those cheap plastic kid's toboggans to tote groceries and laundry. Going downhill fully loaded was interesting, as you can imagine.

Just before Christmas, it was bitter cold and we were burning our wood at a prodigious rate. It was snowing heavily (surprise surprise surprise, said with a Gomer Pyle voice). The snow was too deep to cut any firewood on our land, so I started calling firewood sellers. Everyone was out. I finally got a hold of a kid in Palatine Bridge, a pretty long drive in good weather, but he said he'd be happy to deliver it that day. I gave him very explicit directions to our driveway, adding "Don't worry, it is there. I'll meet you up there, just call me from Caroga Lake (about ten miles away) which is the last place you'll have cell service."

I got the call and hiked up the driveway. It was snowing heavily, and the road wasn't plowed. But through the snow, I saw him coming down the road. It was a crew cab type truck, loaded with wood. Five guys jumped out and started chucking firewood into the driveway. When done, I thanked him, handed him a check, and started loading up the toboggans, along with Pam and our daughter Megan who was staying with us for a time. We started loading up the wood shed attached to the cabin and decided it would be more efficient if Megan stacked and Pam and I tobogganed. Pam decided it would be even more efficient to ride her loaded toboggan down the driveway. It is not easy to steer a toboggan, especially when it is loaded with firewood and you have a precarious perch on top. She capsized several times, which I found pretty funny, as did she.

For the record, we decided that there is no way we're doing that again! We left our town for Florida on January 10th, 2014 in a snowstorm. Later that year, in 2014, we left for Florida in

November. In 2015, probably October. My mamma didn't raise no fool.

Chapter 7: Return from Florida

I won't bore you with our stay in Florida, other than to say that it doesn't snow there. My days were spent fishing, shooting pool on our table in the garage, and saving the world on Facebook with my pithy comments and brilliant political insight.

Our cabin was as we left it, but full of mouse turds again. A job for Sassy, a world champion mouser. It seems the little tramp got out of the RV in Florida before we could get her fixed (which we intended to do) and was pregnant. No, we wouldn't fix her then, and before we knew it, we had three kittens.

Life was normal at the cabin, except for one thing. I lost the use of my right arm for the most part. I saw a neurosurgeon in Guilderland. He did his doctor thing and said my fractured discs hadn't healed properly and surgery was needed. I had the operation, fusing discs C2 through C7 and was ordered not to do any heavy lifting until he cleared me. He also stuck me back in the neck brace from hell. Sigh. So progress on the property was minimal, and I was stuck saving the world on Facebook again. No rock wall building for me. No barn raising. No nothing.

Chapter 8: Our First Foot print

It was August 25, 2014. Pam and I loaded the dogs into the car and headed up our driveway to go over to our property when Pam noticed that the tarp was off our well. I stopped and we checked it out. When I replaced the foot valve on the dug well in the spring, I secured the tarp with rope around the well casing.

The dug well is a large concrete casting, covered on top with particle board, with a large blue tarp over it and with a thick rope encircling it to hold it on.

The rope was pulled off and tossed off to the side, and next to it was the tarp. We couldn't figure out how that happened. We'd had an extended dry spell and the creeks were just trickles. It must have been a bear, I thought. The thick rope holding on the tarp wasn't untied. It was broken. It must have been a bear. Only a bear is strong enough to break a rope this thick, and a large bear at that.

As I was tying the tarp back on, Pam said "Come look at this!". She was pointing to the ground.

"What is it? A bear track?" I asked.

"No. Come look."

I walked over and looked at it. It looked like a human print, but short, and fat.

"That's too small to be a human foot print," I said.

"No, the heel is back here," she replied, as she pointed to a spot way behind a stick.

My jaw dropped. No person makes a foot print that large... and who would be messing around the well anyway... it had to be...

Bigfoot?   But they're not real.   Everyone knows they don't really exist.   Only people with overactive imaginations, or crazy people, or intoxicated people see Bigfoot.   And if they did exist, they only live in the Pacific Northwest, right?

My mind was racing.   What in the world?   First the video... were the Sasquatch groups right?   Was that animal noise a Sasquatch?   Naw... couldn't be.   But yet...

The print was huge, about eighteen to twenty inches long! What's that funny ridge in the middle though?   (Make a mental note of that, I'll get to it later.)

"David!   Here's another one!"

The second was filled with water, and so nothing could be determined from it.   Pam's hand span measures 7 inches (I just measured it. This isn't something one usually knows about a spouse), so that print is about twelve inches. Smaller than the first... two Bigfoots?

I tied the tarp back on, my mind racing.

The well isn't pretty, but it works. It's not my well anyway. I only rent it.

I was numb. After I tied the tarp back on we took the dogs to the property to run. We sat on our deck, having a couple of beers while the dogs played in the woods. Bigfoot? It can't be. What was it?

When we returned to our cabin, I started googling Bigfoot. I also searched for and joined a few Facebook groups.

This isn't a hard and fast rule, but it seems that people who refer to the creature as Bigfoot have only a casual understanding of what it is, while those who called it Sasquatch were more serious about it. If you want to sound cool, you can also call them boogers, a mainly southern term. Yuck. I decided that I was certainly now taking it seriously and would only use the term Sasquatch from here on out.

Chapter 9: Shaking Tree

On the evening of September 6, 2014 I had my DSLR camera set up on its tripod and connected the remote, lockable shutter release. I'm an amateur photographer, and one of my favorite things to photograph are the stars. I'm night blind and that's the only way I get to see them. I usually look at a computer astronomy program to see where interesting things are, like the Milky Way, and then point the camera in that general direction and take a few shots. Then I'll set up for star trail photos, which involves a series of 30 second exposures that get "stacked" to make one photo with long trails. I locked the shutter down and then went into the cabin to watch *Boardwalk Empire* with Pamela. After fifteen minutes or so, I fetched the camera and downloaded the photos to my laptop.

The next morning, I scanned each individual photo before stacking them using special software. They all looked good, clear and crisp, except this one.

Out of 32 photos, this one showed a blurry tree. There was no wind, which means only one thing. It was shaken. It could have been a bear, or a pair of raccoons fighting at the top. Or a Bigfoot, I chuckled to myself.

The next morning, Pam hiked down into the ravine while I stood where the camera had been. She shook several trees.

"Shake the one to the right of that one. That's the one."

"I can't. It's too big."

I hiked down to where she was. The tree was about a foot in diameter, maybe bigger. There were no claw marks as a bear might make. Pam pointed up the tree. Small branches were broken off up around eight feet off the ground.

This is getting creepy, I thought. Last year I heard some odd knocking down here but I wrote it off as a buck knocking velvet off his horns. I need to learn about Bigfoot, and fast. What if they're real? What if they're dangerous? What if I'm insane?

Chapter 10: the Hand Print

September 26, 2014. It was getting pretty around the mountain with the leaves turning. This photo was taken outside the cabin. Yes. We have a view like this all around the cabin. We live in the woods.

I had to run into the city to do something. What, I can't remember. When I got home, I decided to take the dogs to run on our property down the road. They ride in the back of Kia, and when we returned to the cabin and when I reached to open the hatch, there was a hand print. A... big... hand print.

OK, this is getting a little freaky now. I sometimes drive along a dirt road here in town. It is a pretty drive along a country dirt road. As a result, the car gets pretty dusty, especially on the stern. No biggie. We abuse this poor Kia so much anyway.

A paw print? Bear? I took a closeup of one distinct print, and it has the markings of a fingerprint. Do Black Bears have fingerprints like people?

I went back out to show Pam when she got back from refereeing a volleyball game and showed her.

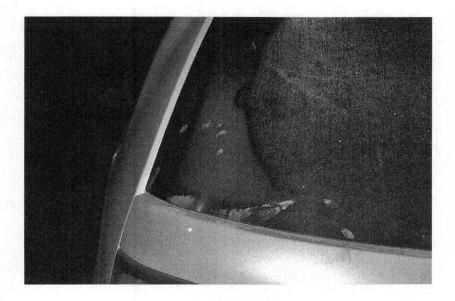

It is a very large palm print. The bottom of the hand is on the lower left part of the back window, then four finger prints above. The strange mark on the lower left is a thumb print, with the thumb being dragged along the glass. Whatever it was must have had very oily or greasy hands to leave something like that.

The bottom pic is a second thumb print to the right of the hand print. Sorry for the reflection from Pam holding a flashlight.

OK, I will say it. I think this is a Sasquatch. No bear, nor any other animal that I know of, could have made that print. It is not human. I have very large hands, and it is much bigger than mine. Something walked behind the car, and for whatever reason, steadied itself on the car as it passed by.

One thing had me baffled though. Those parallel lines on the palm and thumb. On the palm, they're slightly curved. On the thumb, almost perfectly straight. It almost looks like corduroy. That left me scratching my head.

A few of you might be thinking "why didn't you see the print when you put the dogs IN the back of the car?" Two words. Peanut butter. I can't even find the peanut butter in the cabinet, and I know it is there and have a pretty good idea of about where.

Remember I mentioned my superpower of being oblivious to, well, everything?

I was initially a non-believer until finding the foot print, and than I became a skeptic. Now, I'm a believer.

I eagerly posted hand print photos on various Facebook groups and was surprised to learn that not too many people were interested. I was about to learn a lesson about the Bigfoot community.

"Someone is messing with you."

"That's the print from a corduroy jacket" (we don't have corduroy jackets).

"You made that with a snow scraper."

Now, I know there's a lot of baloney on the internet regarding Sasquatch. While I don't believe hoaxes are common, they certainly happen by pranksters and those looking for attention. But I had something pretty solid here, I thought.

If you're a beginning researcher (see, I used another cool Sasquatch term there), take heed. I've learned that a very large percentage of people belonging to Sasquatch groups and organizations are naysayers. I think that is because they want to be the first to produce solid evidence, or perhaps they have a hoity-toity attitude of superiority. If you find yourself joining groups that dismiss clear evidence, or worse yet post photos of blobsquatches (a blurry fuzzy photo of nothing discernible, often with a red circle to show you where to look), consider leaving that group. They aren't serious.

You will also see that if you prove yourself to be serious about the subject, to not be dismissive of everything and to offer interesting evidence yourself, you'll be invited to join secret Sasquatch Facebook groups. Yes, secret. They're secret because they don't want Bigfoot yahoos asking to join. They are by invitation only. I've been invited to several and it is refreshing to be with like minded people. Of course, you have to post in the other groups to be noticed.

So I continued posting my hand print everywhere I could, and spent countless hours looking for a comparison photo and came up empty.

Eventually, a CSI from West Virginia saw it and asked for high resolution copies. After a couple of days, he messaged me on Facebook to tell me that they certainly weren't human, but he couldn't say they were Sasquatch because he has nothing to compare them to.

I felt slightly let down, but I was learning about Sasquatch evidence. If you didn't see what made the hand print or the foot print, or what brushed against the tree and left hair, it is only circumstantial evidence. There has even been supposed Sasquatch DNA found, but upon analysis it is only labeled as unknown, since there is nothing to compare it to.

The best evidence of the existence of Sasquatch is the famous Patterson-Gimlin Film of "Patty" taken in Bluff Creek, California in 1967. Most people back then thought it was a hoax. But today's modern computer technology can enhance and stabilize the film's images. You can see muscles moving under the hair and pendulous breasts, but to most people (like me pre-hand print) it was a man in a suit.

This is disturbing to me. It seems that the only way to prove the existence of Sasquatch is to produce a body. There is a certain percentage that have no problem hunting one and shooting it. But so far, no one has brought one down, even though plenty have shot at them. Many cannot bring themselves to shoot because the Sasquatch face is said to have human qualities.

Why aren't bodies found of Sasquatches that have died of natural causes? Some people theorize that because Sasquatches are people, they bury their dead. Maybe. But how many bodies of anything are found in the forest? I've spent many years in the woods, as a kid, as a hunter, and as a hiker. The Adirondacks have an estimated three to four thousand bears, and I've never seen a dead one. Nature removes bodies very quickly. Scavengers, maggots, and fungus act fast. Depending on weather, it could take anywhere from a couple of weeks to a month before the bear isn't recognizable as a bear.

But why is it necessary to prove the existence of Sasquatch? At this point, I was completely convinced that they are not only real, but that I was living among them. I don't really care if anyone produces a body to validate my beliefs. I've got a foot print, and I've got a hand print. That's proof enough for me.

It seems that the more I learn, the more I don't know.

Chapter 11: Again With The Well.

It was October 3, 2014 and Pam had headed off to work. A few minutes later she stuck her head in the cabin door.

"The tarp is off the well again."

This time, something merely pulled the rope up and over the top of the well. The wooden cover was still in place, so something must have lifted the cover, maybe scooped up a few handfuls of water, and dropped it back on. Eight foot tall hairy man or no, this is getting annoying.

I looked about for foot prints but didn't see anything. That doesn't mean much though. You're probably catching on that I'm not very observant.

I logged onto Amazon and researched Sasquatch and Bigfoot books. I really need to get up to speed here. What are these things? Monsters? Apes? Missing Links? Forest people? Are they dumb animals or intelligent? Why haven't people seen Sasquatches running around? So many questions, so many diverse opinions. Which ones are correct?

Chapter 12: Researching Bigfoot

I ordered several books from Amazon based on Amazon customer reviews and advice from my fellow 'squatchers (note how I used that really cool term there?).

Bigfoot! The True Story of Apes in America by Loren Coleman.

Bigfoot Casebook Updated: Sightings and Encounters from 1818 to 2004 by Janet Bord

Sasquatch: Legend Meets Science by Dr. Jeff Meldrum

Fascinating. A college professor who studies Bigfoot? An anthropologist no less. A casebook with reports going back to 1818, and with over 1,000 reported sightings? A true story? I had a lot to learn. I wanted... no, needed to get up to speed fast.

The first book I read was Meldrum's book. Jeff , a professor at Idaho State University, takes a scholarly approach to Sasquatch. He theorizes that Sasquatch may be *Gigantopithicus*, a ten foot tall ape that lived in Asia but was now extinct. Maybe extinct. Meldrum thinks it is possible that Gigantopithicus crossed the land bridge, just as Native Americans did, and they are not extinct.

I read with fascination about Sasquatch foot print casts. There are many thousands of them (*really?*), of which Meldrum is in possession of not only his own casts, but most of the collection of Dr. Grover Krantz who was also a professor of anthropology at Washington State and who had passed away. In his discussion of the anatomy of the Sasquatch foot, I was amazed at the incredible amount of information can be found from a plaster cast. Meldrum said it is easy to differentiate Sasquatch foot prints from human or hoaxed prints because of a mid-tarsal break. To a layman like me, it basically means there is an added joint in the middle of the foot.

While a human foot only bends at the toe, a Sasquatch bends first at the mid-tarsal joint and then the toes. This sometimes causes dirt to ridge not only at the toe bend, but also in the middle.

Remember this?

About halfway between Pam's pointing index finger and her thumb up by the toes you can see a slight ridge of dirt. I don't know how well this will print in a book, but I hope it is clear. If you can find me on Facebook, I have a public folder of my Sasquatch photos. You're welcome to view them.

Hey! I learned something! Mid-tarsal break. This is a great book and I was enjoying it immensely.

Chapter 13: More Footprints

October 20, 2014 was a glorious day. I took the dogs over to our property that afternoon. As is my habit, I wandered down to the deer trail to look for deer tracks. There was a small set, either a small doe or a fawn. Then I saw these. The first photo isn't that clear. It was better in person. This Sasquatch was also walking up a short hill so the heel prints aren't as distinct as the toes.

The toe prints in the following photo are very distinct.

When I first saw the prints, they were very plainly clear. In the
few minutes I took to fetch my camera, they were fading to what
you see above. They must have been very, very fresh, perhaps
made just minutes before I arrived. By the time Earl, Judi (my in-
laws), and friend Bill came over to see them, they were almost
gone. But in the pics above, if you look carefully, you can see
toes, arched feet, and heels. The top pic is a left foot, the second a
right.

This would be a good time to show you a bear track.

Bears also have toes, but that's where the similarity ends. As you can see, a bear print has rounded toes, whereas Sasquatch have toes like humans, generally straight across. A bear print is also much shorter than a Sasquatch, but there is some confusion because a bear's hind foot sometimes steps at the back of the front foot print, making what might appear to be a large Sasquatch print. Look for toe shape and evidence of claws to determine if what you're seeing is Sasquatch or bear.

Walking back up the hill, I noticed that the bright LED light that burns 24/7 was gone from our screen house. As it turns out, it wasn't gone. Something pulled on the electric cord that leads to it, pulling the light up to the top of the screen.

If you look, you can see the cord running from the top of the screen (under the roof) and to a tree, and from there down to a truck battery kept charged by solar panels. The cord was about seven feet off the ground. No, no footprints there. It was too rocky.

Chapter 14: Footprints and a Baggie

Yep. I've lost it. I'm seeing Sasquatch signs in everything I see now.

October 27, 2014. I took the dogs to our property. It warmed up nicely, the sun was shining, and they needed to run. I let them out of the car and all three bolted over the bank, barking like crazy. So I wandered down there and found the most distinct Sasquatch print yet.

It was big. I later posted this photo on one of my groups, and of course their first question was "How big was it? You did measure it, right??"

"Uh... no. I'm new at this. Am I supposed to?"

"Did you cast it?"

"Sorry no. I'm new to all this stuff."

After taking the above pic, I wandered up to the screen house. Huh. The waste basket that is usually under the table was pulled out. Pulled out and full of rain water, since it rained the night before, so I laid it down to drain the water out. Why would a bear drag a waste basket out from under the table and then not root through it? Then I noticed a baggie laying on the ground nearby. I picked it up. Half a baggie, actually.

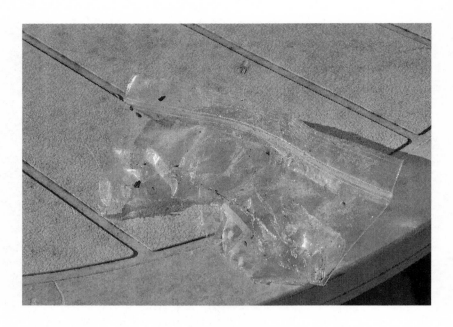

Huh. Raccoon? Coyote? I looked at it closely. No fang marks.
It looks like a huge human-type bite.

You can almost see the tooth marks.

Pam looked at it later (she was reffing a volleyball game) and said she had hamburger in there before tossing it in the waste basket the night before. We barbecued the previous evening.

I leave you to draw your own conclusions.

Chapter 15: Sasquatch's House

It was November 5, 2014, and autumn was departing and winter was approaching. Most all of the leaves were off the trees and there was a nip in the air. We weren't leaving for Florida for a few days. I hoped the snow would hold off.

It was a productive day on the mountain. While Pam trailered Jeremiah the Horse to the vet for a health check, I assembled Bessie the Tractor's frame for its winter tarp. I'd be able to drive into one end of the frame, and then walk the three legs of the tripod, one by one, into position behind her.

The trailer in the background is for storage while we build something. I bought it from a local trucking company the previous year. Earl and I struggled to get it into position there because there was no easy way to get the backhoe back through the brush, but Earl managed it.

Bessie is a 1952 Ferguson TO-30. She has a hydraulic manure bucket on the front and came with a tow bar for the stern. I bought a back blade, a post hole digger, and a gravel scoop for it, all of which can be seen scattered about. One of our first orders of business it to build a pole barn to store that stuff.

This is the view looking up from the game trail. That's Harvey the RV in the photo below, our winter Florida home.

I decided to check the game trail for tracks. Besides dogs, we've seen deer and Sasquatch prints here. Three sets of Sasquatch prints, actually. One set much larger than my size 11, one about the same size, and one smaller. Dad, mom, and kid? As I looked down the trail, I noticed a twisted and broken stick. According to a DVD recently sent to me by a Sasquatch group in Georgia, Sasquatches will sometimes do this to mark trails.

This is it up close. Not too big of a stick, but definitely broken and twisted. But a person could do this. A hand is necessary to twist a branch, something no bear could do. Only a human, or a Sasquatch.

I went just a little farther, and what I found made my jaw drop. Very large saplings were bent over and then covered with small branches, making a little hut of sorts. The large tree in the middle was pushed over, either by the wind or a large Sasquatch, sometime within the past two years. How do I know? There is a green ribbon tied around it. Pam and I marked the trees the loggers were not to cut with these green ribbons. The tree was not cut, but pushed or fallen over. Then smaller saplings were bent over and held with logs and branches, forming a cave of sorts.

The low entrance is in the pic below. Just large enough for something to crawl into to sleep in, or perhaps ambush game passing by, like deer. Our dogs, particularly the pointer, who will climb into anything to look for rodents, wouldn't set foot inside this.

The structure was also very long. Large enough for a Sasquatch family of three, certainly.

The trail split here. To the right were more broken and twisted branches. The photo below shows a classic "tree twist", or more properly a "branch twist". This one is large enough that a human couldn't do it.

But this was the most bizarre. This very large sapling was snapped off, and then bent backwards and held in place by another tree. Look at the diameter of the base of the tree, bottom left. This is well off any trail and actually on state land. It is theorized that, because of the scarcity of food, Sasquatch make unnatural looking things as territory markers.

Another view of the same tree from farther back. The top branches of this tree were also broken and twisted. Could this indeed be some kind of territorial marker? Something obviously made, and not by natural causes? This was on the state land that borders our property.

Besides the massive hand print on the back of our car, these were the most compelling signs I've seen. It is all quite amazing to me, to go from a non-believer to a believer faster than a 427 Cobra can go from zero to 100 MPH.

Chapter 16: The Hand Print

We were back in Florida at this point. Time to really dig into all things Sasquatch.

Since our finding of apparent Sasquatch signs, I'd been studying Sasquatches. Are they real or not? I have books and the internet for research tools, and it is all pretty convincing. Footprints, videos, photos, and audio recordings. But as near as I can tell, there have been thousands of plaster casts made of Sasquatch footprints, but nothing of a hand print except one muddy print many years ago on a woman's door.

Remember this?

I found this print on the back of our car after driving down a dusty dirt road in our town, which covered the stern of the car in dust, effectively dusting for fingerprints.

First, look to the left of the window. See the smudges? Something rubbed up against the side of the car. But that's not it.

Well, look at the base of the thumb in the photo above. See those parallel horizontal lines? Those had me baffled, and kept me from being 100% sure this was from a Sasquatch. What is that?

I had joined a Facebook Sasquatch page, posted that photo, and asked for feedback. About half weren't sure, the other half tried to explain it away as being human, or faked. The lines on the thumb print were thought to be a knit cuff of a jacket.

Well, it wouldn't be a knit cuff. First, the lines go the wrong way. Secondly, this was September. We don't wear winter jackets with knit cuffs in September. Besides, there was also a second thumb print to the right of this one, with the same marks.

I was at the end of Dr. Jeff Meldrum's excellent book, *Sasquatch: Legend Meets Science* and I got to the chapter on hand and foot prints. Meldrum asserts that Sasquatches aren't human, of course. He believes they are a type of North American Ape. In talking about the plaster casts of Sasquatch foot prints, he says that casts of the real ones (as opposed to the hoaxes) often have dermal ridges, like finger prints. Apes also have "friction skin" he said that aids them in climbing. Coarse, heavy ridges. Friction Skin are found on the soles of feet and the palms of hands of apes. PALMS OF HANDS!! FRICTION SKIN!! THAT'S IT!!

Now, there is no doubt in my mind whatsoever that we had at least one, but I suspect a family of Sasquatches living by us. The hand print is the most convincing bit of evidence I've seen. Presented here are several other photos.

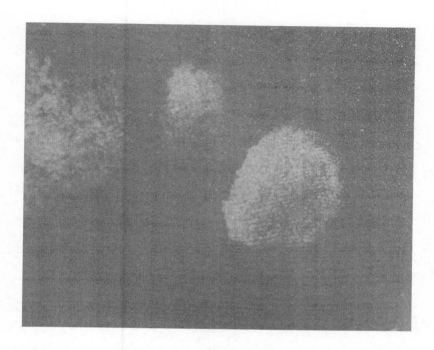

Above, fingerprints, notice no whorls in these.

Below, night photos taken when I showed Pam the prints.

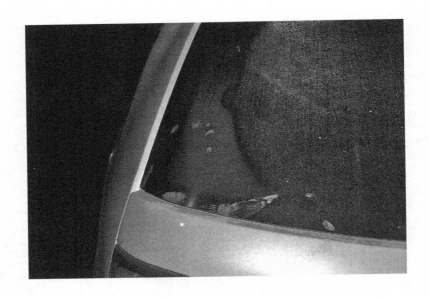

Granted, the prints are strange, and I can understand the corduroy thing, but no. Just no.

Chapter 17: The Research Continued in Florida

Wearing the neck brace most of the summer of 2014, I couldn't get much of anything done on the property. I tried building a small rock wall using rocks weighing less than five pounds, but it looked silly. So I spent most of my time surfing Al Gore's internets trying to learn about Sasquatch. When we migrated to Florida with the rest of the snowbirds, I had almost as much time. I say almost, because we have a pool table here that I use for "physical therapy" for my bum right arm.

Regarding the hand print, I posted it everywhere I could, and no one had anything to compare it to, so it couldn't be confirmed as to what it was. A CSI in West Virginia asked for high resolution copies of the photos. He couldn't say it was a Sasquatch, but he could say that it wasn't human. I thought I was at a dead end.

I then decided to send it to published researchers. I'm sure these guys are hammered by people sending them photos asking for validation, but they were my last resort. One, who I won't name yet, immediately replied to my email query and said that he had other Sasquatch hand prints and it looked like a match. He asked for high resolution versions, which I sent. He then forwarded them to a forensic anthropologist in San Francisco who was very excited and "very impressed" with them. This researcher asked if he could publish it in his next book, to which I agreed. So to me, I've done my homework on that print. It is the best I could do without actually seeing what made the print.

As for the vocalization, I did the same thing. I posted it everywhere, asking what it might be. I played every supposed Sasquatch audio I could find and nothing matched. I went back to coyotes, foxes, and owls like the hunters suggested. The audio I played got no response from my dogs. Or from me for that matter, because it didn't sound anything like what I had recorded. When I found the Umatilla vocalizations, which were supposedly made by a Sasquatch, I had a match (Umatilla is an Indian reservation). I then found a Native American Sasquatch group, joined, and posted it there, asking for opinions. The quick and resounding response was that it was a Sasquatch imitating a coyote, most likely in an attempt to lure my dogs into the woods. This explanation makes sense to me.

What I've learned about Sasquatch vocalizations so far, discounting the talking Sasquatches, is that they are very ape-like. They whoop, they chatter, and they whistle. Yes, whistle like a human. If you look at photos of totem poles in the Pacific Northwest, you'll see depictions of Sasquatch heads, and many have their lips shaped in a circle as if whistling. Go ahead, google it. You know you want to. I'll wait.

I've also been told by Native Americans that the Forest People can imitate animal vocalizations. This makes me wonder if Native Americans learned to do this from Sasquatches, or vice-versa.

Practically all Native American tribes have legends of the Forest People, even tribes with no contact with each other. They refer to them by various names and consider them as another Indian tribe. They also say they are cannibals. This has me somewhat concerned, although so far, they've let me and Pam be.

If you look at the video of my vocalization, you won't see my two pit bulls. The male was cowering on the couch and the female was hiding under a table. Only the mighty hunting dog would venture outside. This German Shorthaired Pointer free ranges through the forest and has been captured on a trail cam a half mile from our cabin, but she wouldn't go 100 feet from the cabin in this instance. Since dogs will investigate what they don't know, I believe they must have had their own Sasquatch encounter and are well aware of what it was.

To me, these two things are not solid evidence, but are pretty compelling. Enough so to make a skeptic ponder the existence of Sasquatch. I've done my due diligence on those two pieces of evidence. I could also post other pics, but they really don't show anything. Take the photo of the baggie that was pulled out of a garbage can. It had remnants of hamburger in it. The bottom of the baggie was bitten off in what looks like one huge bite. What does it prove? Not much. I've got clear photos of foot prints, and of the tree being shaken when I was taking star photos. But it is not really convincing evidence of anything. It is only when taken in totality that it becomes convincing, at least to me.

So we started 2014 as Sasquatch non-believers, and ended as Sasquatch believers. The last step is Sasquatch knowers. What would 2015 at our cabin in the woods hold for us?

Chapter 18: Pamela's Sasquatch Dream

The other day, Pamela told me about a dream she had about Sasquatch. She said it was one of the most vivid dreams she's ever had. I thought two things. First, that it was an interesting dream, as dreams most always are. Second, there is a small percentage of believers who think Sasquatch are a more advanced life form than humans, and they are telepathic. Now, I don't think that, but hey. I thought Sasquatches didn't exist for me up until a few months ago, so who knows? We're down in sunny Florida as I write this, far far away from our Sasquatches.

I asked her to write it down to be included with this book. This is Pamela's Sasquatch dream.

My dream

Dreams are strange. I have some strange ones. Most recently I dreamt of Sasquatch. Bigfoot.... Real? The dream sure was....dreams are funny. Some things are very familiar, not necessarily real, but familiar. He first approached me outside. The property felt like someplace I had lived before but it had an out building that shouldn't be there. The Squatch was watching me and following me. Then I was talking to it. I said I wanted to hide it and it showed me how it had been staying in the out building. Then it agreed to meet some people to prove it was real. Next we were someplace else and there were a dozen or so people there. The building wasn't home but a regular building. Homey but it had a square bar. Almost felt like Vrooman's *(an old Adirondack restaurant and hotel - Dave)*.

The Squatch was shy but trying to be social. More and more people coming in. I asked him if he hit Dave with the tree. He said he didn't hit Dave with a tree. He didn't.

There was a white Sasquatch tending bar. She seemed young, like maybe teenage aged. Very white, very shy, very sweet. She said "We're all born white." Then I had a small white puppy *(baby Sasquatch – Dave)* in my hands. So small, so sweet. Then I had a brown one. She had a tear roll down her face when she said she never changed to a darker color. Next Squatch was outside with me. He said things were scary....he was very shy, he was afraid for the pups and he wanted to leave when a car pulled up . My brother and his wife Tracy got out and said the pups were ugly. I was defending my pups and the Squatches when my alarm went off.

Chapter 19: Sasquatches in South Carolina

May 4th, 2015; We're now in upstate New York, arriving here from Florida. It took a week to make the trip. We travel slowly because Pam was towing Jeremiah, her horse. Traveling with a horse, nine dogs (including mother-in-law Judi's), three cats, and two rabbits means that we can't stay at a motel like normal people. We stay at ranches, farms, and hunting preserves.

Our first stop was in Allendale, South Carolina at a 2,600 acre hunting preserve. It isn't hunting season and so we decided to stay a couple of days so Pam could ride the trails. When she returned from her first ride, she was very excited.

"There are Sasquatch signs everywhere! Especially tree bends! And I think I even heard one whoop and then grunt at me! I'm going back out with my camera!"

I now know that Sasquatches are found all over North America and live in all North American states. All they want is forest, food, and water. This hunting preserve is forested. It is rich with deer, wild pigs, and who knows what else. And there is plenty of water. Everyplace that there was water, Pam saw Sasquatch tree bends. This one was the most impressive to me. Two saplings were bent over and then pinned down by breaking a third. That break in the pinning tree is about ten feet off the ground.

It is theorized that unnatural tree bends are territory markers to warn other Sasquatches (and now me) to stay away. The photo above is the most impressive, but there were others nearby, such as this one.

As you can see, the pinning tree has leaves. It was perfectly thriving and happy.

Sometimes, trees are broken just for fun, I think. This break is also about eight or ten feet above the ground.

I posted these photos on a Sasquatch Facebook page I frequent. One person replied and said that there have been nine Sasquatch sightings in Allendale in the past two years. I couldn't verify this, but from all of the signs Pam found, I certainly wouldn't doubt it.

Chapter 19: Sasquatches in Virginia

After an overnight at a ranch in Charlotte, North Carolina, we were next staying at a riding campground called Fort Valley Ranch in the George Washington National Forest. This is another of Pam's favorite places and so we decided to stay two days here so she could ride. And, as I expected, Pam came back very excited.

"I found all kinds of tree bends!" she gushed. "Only they were all single trees bent and pinned."

This time she had brought her camera, and so didn't need to ride back out. She rode with three folks from a nearby campsite. When Pam explained why she was taking photos of seemingly nothing to most people, they all looked at her dubiously.

"Those occur naturally. I see that all the time," said one lady.

Exactly! Only they don't always occur naturally. These creatures are everywhere.

If you get into the subject of Sasquatches, you will quickly learn that only about 15% of Americans believe they exist. Most people, as I was until the summer of 2014, think it is bunk. So if you are a sensitive type, you might want to choose your audience carefully when discussing Sasquatches. Or, if you are like me and don't really care a whit what anyone thinks of you, talk about Sasquatches with total strangers. You might get a kick out of their reactions. I know I do.

Chapter 21: Gifting

Once you get immersed in the subject of Sasquatches, you'll quickly realize that there is a culture that has grown up around it. People who claim to live among them, as do I, also sometimes claim to interact with them. They are referred to as habituators.

The wildest stories are from people who claim to talk to them and even know their names. My Sasquatch beliefs are still evolving and I try my best to keep an open mind, but I still file these stories under "C" for crazy.

Many habituators "gift". That is, they leave food and trinkets at a designated gifting spot for their Sasquatch, who take them. Sometimes the Sasquatch will leave something in exchange, anything from fish to marbles. Marbles, you ask? Yes. That is the claim. File this under "C".

Personally, I think gifting is a bad idea. Sort of like when Pam gave that big black bear the gift of sunflower seeds. We put the seeds in the wood shed and locked it. A few days later, the door was covered in scratches that looked like bear claws. An old friend of mine had a similar problem with a bear and his bird seed, and he too removed the feeders and put them in a shed. The next day, the shed door was ripped off. Do you really want to get an eight foot, eight hundred pound critter angry because you didn't gift him with food or trinkets?

Chapter 22: Game Cameras

I'm sure that many of you reading this are wondering why there aren't better photographs of Sasquatch. The best is the Patterson-Gimlin film of 1967 which shows "Patty" calmly walk away from the camera as she sashays, looking back over her shoulder (which is something apes cannot do, by the way) at Roger Patterson. As an aside, if you are a cool 'Squatcher, you refer to the Patterson-Gimlin Film simply as PGF. There are also many other clear photos of Sasquatch, but they are too distant to be confirmed as much of anything.

"But what of game cameras?" you ask, and rightly so. "With all the game cameras around, why hasn't anyone got a good photo?"

Good question. I put up a game camera in 2014 and all Sasquatch activity immediately ceased. I was baffled. I moved the camera around to different locations and checked it daily for about two weeks. The best I got was my dogs.

Doing what I always do when presented with a problem, I turned to Al Gore's internets for possible answers. One came back immediately. Sasquatch can sense the camera's infrared light, or perhaps electronic noise, or maybe just sense that something is out of place in its forest.

Many species can see colors and light that we humans cannot. Sasquatch are said to reflect red eye shine at night, and that this might be a clue. Not to me. As a photographer, I sometimes have to deal with "red eye" when using a flash. Many computer programs even have a red eye removal tool. To me, this simply means that a Sasquatch eye is human-like.

Others theorize that Sasquatches know their forest, and are quick to spot anything out of the ordinary, like electronics attached to a tree pointed at a game trail. They simply walk around it.

Habituators claim that Sasquatches know what a camera is, and don't like having their picture taken. File this under "C".

But for the record, I have found trail cam photos online of creatures that don't look like bears, but they are all too grainy and indistinct to be of any value. At least to me.

Chapter 23: Hit by a tree

If you recall, in an earlier chapter I related the story of me cutting down a tree and then getting hit by a leaner from the left. It was a small sapling, but big enough to knock me silly and break my neck. Everyone who looked at the tree I cut, and the one that hit me, couldn't believe it.

"What are the odds of that?" they'd ask.

Pretty long.   But it did.

One night, Pamela and I were discussing Sasquatch. I am the researcher, and I sometimes impart what I've learned to Pamela. We were discussing the nest, or possible hunting blind that I'd found on our property, not too far down the hill and on a game trail.

"How far from the nest is the tree you cut down?" asked Pamela.

"I dunno. Between fifty and a hundred feet."

"Didn't you say that Sasquatch use rocks and trees as weapons?"

"According to the Iroquois, and an ancient Etruscan plate I found in an old anthropology book, yes."

"Maybe the tree that hit you wasn't a leaner.   Maybe you made our Sasquatch mad when you cut a tree close to his house."

We laughed and laughed.

Chapter 24: File Under "C"

As with any topic on the paranormal, Sasquatch has its share of nuts.

First, let me say that there are no experts on the topic of Sasquatch. No one has produced a body or captured one, and no one has studied them in the field, as Jane Goodall does Chimpanzees. While there are ten thousand reported sightings, no one knows much of anything about them. But that doesn't keep people from claiming to know all about them.

For example, some believe that there is a correlation between UFO sightings and Sasquatch sightings. Therefore, it is logical to assume that the two are connected. Sasquatches come from outer space in UFOs.

Some believe that Sasquatches are inter-dimensional, which is how they seemingly vanish into thin air. They pass into another dimension using portals. Orange portals are for Sasquatches and blue ones are for UFOs.

Why are most all photos of Sasquatches blurry? Why do many photos require a red circle to show you where the Sasquatch is? Because a Sasquatch can mess with your electronics using special powers.

Yep. That's it.

To me, the biggest problem facing a beginning researcher is separating the wheat from the chaff. If you're open minded enough to believe Sasquatches might exist, why can't they be inter-dimensional? Common sense, I guess. That, and no other creature that we know of is inter-dimensional. Of course, how would we know?

I guess I tend to use the "how do you know" challenge. How do you know they use portals, or can unfocus your camera, or turn into orbs? Any kind of a theory about Sasquatch is either wild speculation, or something that must be a provable hypothesis with results that can be duplicated by your peers. Otherwise, you're just making stuff up.

Then again, there are things I've learned in 2015 that I thought were total bunk in 2014. I'll explain in later chapters.

Chapter 25: Sasquatch Signs

Now you're all set to run off into the forest to look for Sasquatch. There is little likely-hood that you'll actually see one. And if you do, he will use his special powers to mess with your electronics so any photos you take will be blobsquatches. What do you look for?

Well, the obvious thing is footprints. An eight hundred pound ape is going to leave impressive footprints in soft soil and mud. But what if the forest floor is covered in leaf litter, or very rocky? What else can you do to find if Sasquatches are present?

The very first thing I heard in 2013 were tree knocks. I heard a knocking sound when indoors in our cabin, only I assumed it must have been a buck knocking velvet off his horns. Knowing what I know now, I doubt that. It was, quite simply, too loud. Sasquatch will take a tree branch and strike a tree with it. With the right hardwood tree, it sounds like a baseball bat hitting a hard ball.

No one can say with certainty what tree knocks mean. Some think it must be a form of communications between Sasquatches. Some say it is like a Morse code, and Sasquatch can "talk" to each other, like Native Africans did with drums. Some say it is a warning to stay away. Some say it is to announce the presence of humans in the forest, with one knock per person. Since I wasn't in the woods at the time, and I doubt anyone else was nearby, I filed that one under "C".

Lacking suitable trees and branches, Sasquatches will also knock by hitting two rocks together.

Speaking of rocks, Sasquatch are also famous for throwing them. They're expert throwers, but no one has ever been hit with one, to my knowledge. They toss them to warn humans to stay away. If you don't vacate the premises, they'll strike a bit closer, and then closer, until you get the message.

Speaking of rock throwing, at one point over the winter I decided that I'd been reading too much Sasquatch stuff. I was overdosing. I had bought a used anthropology book and decided to read that. On page one of chapter one was a photo of an Etruscan plate, meaning it dates anywhere from 700 BC to 300 AD.

On the outer frieze (towards the bottom) of this silver bowl a great ape is portrayed, erect and armed. (Detail in drawing below)

:arliest evi-
rilized man

The author states that the figure throwing a rock and wielding a tree branch is an ape. Does that look like an ape to you? Nope. Me neither.

Another obvious sign are tree bends, discussed earlier. If you find a tree bend, look at how the end is pinned. Could it have happened naturally, such as a falling tree branch? Or does the object pinning the bend look placed?

Structures are also easy to find, being somewhat large. It is generally an arrangement of large sticks and small trees to form

89

various shapes such as tee-pees and pyramids. Theories about what these could be vary from territory markers to hunting blinds.

Another notable sign is a horizontal placement of a large stick or branch. When sticks and branches fall, they generally do so in a haphazard manner and wind up laying on the ground or laying up against something. Seeing a perfectly balanced horizontal stick or branch means Sasquatch. Pam and I suspect they might be trail or direction markers.

Speaking of trail markers, Pam and I found what we call "the Sasquatch Highway" which travels past our rental cabin and up the mountain to a remote lake. The trail is extremely easy to follow because of all the tree bends, structures, and directional markers. You certainly don't need to be an expert tracker to follow these. You only need to be observant. I just follow Pam.

Chapter 26: Favorite Stories

I've literally read many hundreds, if not thousands of Sasquatch encounter reports and news articles. My favorite is this one.

A young boy was walking barefoot down a dirt road, heading home. In each hand was a dead chicken. Suddenly, a giant Sasquatch stepped out of the woods and approached the boy, who was frozen in fear. The Sasquatch said nothing, but pointed to the chickens. The boy nervously handed the two chickens to the Sasquatch. The Sasquatch took one, handed one back to the boy, turned, and walked back into the forest.

Possibly the most intriguing (and to possibly file under "C") was the case of Canadian lumberjack Albert Ostman. In 1924, Ostman was camping in British Columbia. He was suddenly snatched from the ground in his sleeping bag and found himself being carried by something off into the forest. Ostman was later deposited at a Sasquatch camp, which consisted of two older Sasquatch and two young. Ostman was held there for several days. He made good his escape by giving his snuff to the old male, who ate it and became ill, giving Ostman his opportunity to escape.

But perhaps the most striking of all is the classic tale of Ape Canyon in the state of Washington near Mount St. Helens, home of the storied mountain gorillas, or mountain devils. What is interesting in this is not only the testimony of what happened by those who experienced it, but the details recorded by the newspaper *Oregonian* of the events of July, 1924.

Five men- Fred Beck, Gabe Lefever, John Peterson, Marion Smith, and his son Roy Smith had been prospecting by Mount St. Helens for several years. Near their claim was a creek where the miners would wash their dishes and fetch drinking water. In 1922, they discovered large human-like footprints near the stream. As time passed, they found many prints, the largest measuring nineteen inches.

The miners gave up their tent and built a small cabin. It had no windows and only one door, and a metal roof. The gaps between the logs were chinked with mud. Building this cabin would prove to be a most fortuitous decision.

After building the cabin, when working their gold claim the men would hear a "thudding, hollow thumping noise". They could not find the cause, and some believed it was one of them playing tricks.

In July of 1924, the men heard a piercing whistle from a nearby ridge. An answering whistle was heard a distance away. Unnerved, the men started carrying their guns with them at all times.

Fred and Marion were fetching water. Marion suddenly shouted and raised his gun. Fred looked up. There, across the creek, was a seven foot tall ape-like creature watching them. It ducked behind a tree. When it peeked around the tree to look at the two men, Fred fired three shots, hitting the tree but missing the Sasquatch. The creature ran off. Fred saw it about 200 yards away and fired three more shots before it disappeared.

Fred and Marion hurried back to the cabin. Night was approaching. The men decided to leave, but did not want to hike back to their car in darkness and decided to wait until morning.

At midnight, the men were awakened by a loud THUMP on the side of the cabin, which knocked some of the mud chinking out of the logs. Looking out, the men could see three Sasquatches, but from the sound of footsteps there were many more. The men decided not to shoot at them unless the cabin was attacked to show that they would defend themselves. Rocks began hitting the cabin. Sasquatches began pounding on the cabin door, which was braced with a board from one of their beds. The men riddled the door with gunfire. Sasquatches climbed on the roof in an attempt to batter it in. The men fired through the roof. The attacks continued all through the night, with periods of quiet.

During one attack, an arm reached through the gap in the chinking and grabbed an ax. Fred lunged for the ax, turning it vertical so it couldn't be pulled through. Marion shot at it and the creature dropped the ax and pulled his hand back.

Shortly before daybreak the attacks ended. At sunrise, the men cautiously emerged from the cabin, then gathered their things and made their way towards their car. Then, about eighty yards away, the men saw a Sasquatch watching them. Fred took careful aim and shot it three times. It toppled over the edge of a canyon.

The men left, leaving their cabin, gear, and supplies. They never returned.

Chapter 27: Where are the bodies?

If Sasquatch exist, why no bodies? Surely, someone would find the remains of one, or shoot one while hunting, or hit it with a car, right?

This is, without a doubt, the main reason the vast majority of people are skeptical of the existence of Sasquatch. Actually, there has been a body, the Minnesota ice man. This story will be told in the next chapter.

Believers readily explain away the lack of bodies. Habituators claim that Sasquatch bury their dead, just like people do. Large holes are easily dug by several Sasquatches and the deceased dropped in and covered. They've seen them do it, they say.

While "Bigfoot" is not one solitary animal, there aren't millions of them either. To have a sustainable reproducing population, the experts calculate that there are thousands of them. The most quoted number I've read is ten thousand.

In New York State, where I've found most of our Sasquatch evidence, there are an estimated six thousand bears. I've never found a bear skeleton. Heck, I've never found any skeletons in the forest. The elements, scavengers, maggots, and fungi make quick work of a dead animal.

Sasquatches are reclusive. They don't want to be around people and prefer remote sections of forest to live. That being said, it is little surprise that if one died, the chances of a person finding the body are slim, especially if they sense their impending demise and wander off to the deep forest to await death.

So no, there are no bodies. Surely one will turn up sooner or later. I'm convinced of that. But what will it prove? That we Sasquatch believers and knowers are right and everyone else is wrong? To be honest, for the sake of Sasquatch, I hope a body is never found and that they are left in peace.

Besides, to me it is much more fun to know something that 85% of people don't believe exists. I know something you don't know, ha ha.

Chapter 28: the Minnesota Iceman

There are many mysterious circumstances concerning the Minnesota Iceman. An unnamed millionaire came to own what, for all intents and purposes, was the body of a type of Sasquatch. The millionaire wanted to exhibit the creature to gauge people's reactions to it. He did not want it to fall into the hands of scientists who might destroy it in examining it. He also did not want to discredit Biblical creation.

The millionaire wanted to exhibit his iceman but keep the news of it relatively quiet. He decided to show the body, which was encased in ice, around America's heartland's rural towns. In 1967, college zoology major Terry Cullen paid twenty-five cents to see the iceman and was impressed with what he saw. For the next year, Cullen tried unsuccessfully to interest college anthropologists. Finally, Cullen contacted noted Sasquatch researcher Ivan Sanderson. By chance, Sanderson was being visited by Belgian cryptozoologist Bernard Heuvelmans.

In December of 1968, both men traveled to the Midwest and spent three days examining the body through the ice. It was a male, about six feet tall. It was covered in hair three to four inches long. It had been shot through an eye, which was missing, and the other eye was dangling out of its socket. Part of the ice had melted exposing some of the flesh, and the two men could smell the stench of putrefaction. After three days of examination, Sanderson and Heuvelmans agreed that it was authentic.

Heuvelmans wrote about the Minnesota Iceman in *the Bulletin of the Royal Institute of National Science of Belgium.*

> The specimen at first looks like a man, or if you prefer, an adult human being of the male sex, of

rather normal height (six feet) and proportions but
excessively hairy. It is entirely covered with very
dark brown hair three to four inches long. Its skin
appears waxlike, similar in color to the cadavers of
white men not tanned by the sun... The specimen is
lying on its back... the left arm is twisted behind the
head with the palm of the hand upward. The arm
makes a strange curve, as if it were that of a sawdust
doll, but this curvature is due to the open fracture
midway between the wrist and the elbow where one
can distinguish the broken ulna in a gaping wound.
The right arm is twisted and held tightly against the
flank, with the head spread palm down over the
right side of the abdomen. Between the right finger
and the medius the penis is visible, lying obliquely
on the groin. The testicles are vaguely
distinguishable at the juncture of the thighs.

In May of 1969, after he and Heuvelmans nicknamed the creature
"Bozo", Sanderson wrote the following for *Argosy:*

Bozo's face is most startling feature, both to
anthropologists and anyone else- and for several
reasons. Unfortunately, both eyeballs have been
"blown out" of their sockets. One appears to be
missing, but the other seems (to some, at least) to be
just visible under the ice. This gives Bozo a
gruesome appearance, which is enhanced by a
considerable amount of blood diffused from the
sockets through the ice. The most arresting feature
of the face is the nose. This is large but only fairly
wide, and is distinctly "pugged", rather like that of a
Pekinese dog- but not like that of a gorilla, which
actually doesn't have a nose, per se. The nostrils are
large, circular and point straight forward, which is
very odd. The mouth is only fairly wide and there is

no eversion of the lips; in fact, the average person would say he had no lips at all. His "muzzle" is no more bulging, prominent, or pushed forward than is our own; not at all prognarhous like that of a chimp. One side of the mouth is slightly agape and two small teeth can be seen. These should be the right upper canine and the first premolar. The canine or eye-tooth is very small and in no way exaggerated into a tusk, or similar to that of a gorilla or a chimp. But- to me, at least- the most interesting features of all are some folds and wrinkle lines around the mouth just below the cheeks. These are absolutely human, and are like those seen in a heavy-jowled, older white man.

The Minnesota Iceman is a continuing mystery. At some point in 1969, the original body was replaced with a copy made in Hollywood. Although similar in appearance, Sanderson's and Heuvelmans' careful three day analysis showed that they could tell the copy from the original body.

Why was the body replaced? The exhibitor would not say why, nor does anyone know where the original is. Perhaps it was destroyed in an accident, or hopefully stored away to preserve it. Remember this story, and watch the news for the reappearance of the Minnesota Iceman.

Chapter 29:   The Iroquois Stone Giants

Most, if not all Native American tribes have described the "hairy forest people". They're described by various names.   The Iroquois, who lived in this area, called theirs "Stone Giants". They were said to rub pine resin all over their bodies and then roll in sand, giving them the appearance of stone.

Many think Sasquatch did this to create a sort of armor to fend off spears and arrows. Not quite, I think. Sasquatch did this to fend off the Adirondack black flies and mosquitoes!

The Stone Giants were said to be extremely aggressive and used rocks and uprooted or broken trees as weapons.   Trees as weapons... remember my "accident"? Remember the Etruscan plate?

Seeing as Sasquatches are so huge, you wouldn't think they'd need rocks and trees to defend themselves. But many Native Americans claim that Sasquatches will fight among themselves, and so rocks and trees would generally be a good idea.

As for my accident, why would a giant Sasquatch smack me with a tree? Maybe he thought I was icky and used a tree for the same reason that we swat bugs with magazines.

Chapter 30: Back in the Adirondacks

We arrived in upstate New York Sunday afternoon, May 3rd, 2015 at my mother-in-law's house. I was beat from driving our RV for seven hours. It is an old RV and a real handful. The cats needed to get to the cabin we rent a mile away and Pam decided to deliver them and to check on everything. On her return, she said that not only was everything good, but better than what she expected. She had put dryer sheets in the drawers and around the cabin and it kept the mice away. We had one dead mouse in the empty garbage can, and one drowned mouse in the toilet. That was it.

Monday morning, I reluctantly arose, ate breakfast, and then Pam and I, and the dogs drove to the cabin. I flipped on the power, except for the electric hot water heater so as not to burn out the element, and primed the pump to get water flowing. This process takes a bit of time, but an hour later it was done. In the meanwhile, Pam was out in the woods looking for signs of Sasquatch. She was not disappointed. She saw many bent trees weighed down by logs and other trees, and even found a faint footprint in the creek by the cabin.

We were standing outside the cabin and I followed Pam as she walked to the side yard. There, right next to the cabin, I found this.

"Pamela?"

"Yes?"

"Did you not see this? You just walked right past it."

"What? Isn't that our Christmas tree from last year?"

"We weren't here for Christmas last year. We were in Florida."

This wasn't here on Sunday. But it was on Monday. It happened Sunday night after Pam left, meaning that the Sasquatch were watching her as she deposited the cats in the cabin.

These were all very small trees. The largest pine tree was two inches in diameter, and it was twisted and broken. A very small pine tree next to it was also snapped right off. A tiny hardwood tree was bent over.

And, for the first time, I found twisted pricker tree branches. See the photo below.

103

There are many forest animals which can break trees. Black bears among them, and we have plenty. But to grab a pine tree or a pricker bush and twist it requires a hand that grasps. Bears don't have hands. Only humans and apes have hands.

I posited that this could be one of two things. It was either a trail marker, meaning that the Sasquatch are moving, most likely to the lake up the mountain from us, and are leaving signs for others to follow. Great. We have a Sasquatch highway in our yard.

Or, it could be a warning.

I posted this on Facebook and a friend said that maybe it was like a bouquet of roses to say "welcome back!"

I hope so!

Chapter 31: Holy Effin' Crap

Tuesday, May 5, 2015; I copied and pasted this from a post Pamela made on Facebook.

HOLY EFFIN CRAP!!! Ok, the sun is coming up and in FL that doesn't happen until about 7am in the spring. So I'm up with the sun.... But it's only 5:30. I get up and both Ruby and Olivia want out for morning potty. Well I know Olivia is going to go running and barking so I stick her on a leash to keep her from doing that and let Ruby out while walking Olivia. I figure I might as well look for footprints since it's so early. What do I find? Another handprint on our car!!! A bigfoot handprint! Only it's much smaller than the one from last year. And it's fresh! Like morning dew in the air fresh! Holy crap... Dogs inside! My heart is racing. Do I wake up David? It's 5:30. He never gets up before 9. Too bad, I have to tell him, so I run upstairs and frantically tell him there's a handprint. He groggily says take a picture.... So I run back downstairs, grab his camera and go creeping outside. I have my back to the wooded pines and briars near the car and try to get a good angle for the photo. I clicked one shot, two shots... The hair on the back of my neck prickles and then heavy thudding footfalls are behind me! Holy crap! What the hell is that??? My brain screams bigfoot! Run! So I ran back in the cabin and up the stairs again. My heart is pounding out of my chest and I'm shaking from head to toe! "David! David! Get up! I had an underwear changing moment! He's out there! I heard him!" So now poor David is up, not awake and pulling on his jeans and tee shirt. I open the door to go back out and Leo the cat comes racing in with a scared look and bounds straight up the stairway never slowing down. I'm standing inside the screen door on our little porch waiting for David and just looking and listening when a black shrouded head drops from view behind a small stand of pines not more than twenty yards in front of me! Now I'm whisper-yelling "I saw it! Right there!" Pointing to the stand of trees. David goes strolling out yelling at it that he's pissed and it needs to come here right now! I told him not to piss it off or it might smack him with a tree again.... So now, with reenforcements behind me, I wander up the driveway a little looking for footprints. Nothing.... Rats. Dave goes back to the car and we examine the handprint more closely. Much smaller than the one from last year. I said "uh oh.... David, if this is a young one, that means there's a mamma around somewhere. We all know how mamma anything can be if it feels it's young is in danger." Ugggh.... Now we will need to be extra vigilant about the dogs. Hopefully the bigfoot family are good hunters and catch wild prey regularly or else my pets are going to be their dinner.

Here is the print that Pamela found on our car's back window. It is much smaller than even Pam's hand. It is too bad that it is not as detailed as an adult's.

A casual observation; humans tend to flatten their palms on things, such as Kia hatches when shutting them. All of the prints that we've found and attributed to Sasquatch are cupped, not flattened.

On close examination of the print, we saw that there was also an adult print. It is only the base of the palm and thumb, and it was very indistinct so it must have gently brushed the window as it passed.

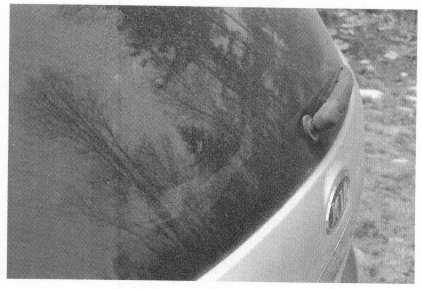

I zoomed in on the thumb. On last year's photo, the friction skin was so thick that it looked like corduroy. The juvenile didn't have such skin except very faintly on the thumb. It makes me wonder if the heavy friction skin is the result of lifting heavy objects, or climbing, just as people get blisters.

But definitely two prints. One adult, one child. I hope it shows well in the book. If not, find me on Facebook, dave_gibson.7355, and look for my Sasquatch book photo album.

I know the photo above is difficult to see in print. It is a photograph of two hand prints. On the bottom is a large adult. On top of that one is a much smaller hand print, presumably a juvenile.

Chapter 32: Sasquatch Groups

I don't know how many Sasquatch groups there are on the internet, but it is a lot. Some are research organizations that look for Sasquatches, evidence, and interview witnesses. Some are habituation sites. Some are silly. Some are good, some are not.

I contacted one recently named the Northern Sasquatch Research Society. It is headed up by Bill Brann who lives in the Whitehall, New York area, a place with a lot of sightings. The TV show *Finding Bigfoot* was there recently to interview folks. The most recent film makers to visit, as of this writing, was by an indie film crew who interviewed witnesses about the 1976 Sasquatch sighting seen by several police officers for their Small Town Monsters documentary *the Beast of Whitehall*.

What makes Bill Brann's group special is Bill Brann. Bill is a serious researcher and organizer. He was at the Abair Road (Whitehall) sighting a couple of days after it occurred to interview witnesses and record their testimony.

This proved to be invaluable to the makers of *the Beast of Whitehall*. I had been in contact with Seth Breedlove, the film's director previously. Seth was having trouble finding witnesses as many wouldn't speak to him, and many had died. I gave him Bill's telephone number. Bill saved the day for Seth by being able to provide detailed accounts of what happened that day. If you turn out to be a serious researcher, this would be a good group to join, if you're a joiner.

The largest and most famous is the Bigfoot Field Research Organization, or BFRO. They have arguably the largest collection of sighting reports assembled. You can view these reports online. The BFRO has many state branches that organize expeditions to "find Bigfoot".

You may be interested in joining expeditions, as my wife Pam is. I am not. I have absolutely no interest. Why? Are you going to see tree bends, footprints, or markers? Maybe, but I've already seen them. Are you going to see a Sasquatch? No. But what you will have is a nice walk in the woods and getting together with others who have a similar interest as you. If I ever go on an expedition, I will be the one who stays behind and tends the campfire.

I don't put much stock in sighting reports as a gauge of Sasquatch activity. Why? To have a sighting, you need two things; a Sasquatch, and someone to see it. My hunch is that Sasquatches are everywhere there is forest, food, water, and not too many people. As I wrote earlier, my town has 38,000 acres and 550 residents, or 69 acres per person. The Adirondack Park is 6.1 million acres and about 100,000 residents, or 61 acres per person. Few people, few sightings.

Face book is loaded with groups. Most are pretty bad, but some are good. The problem with Facebook is that "trolls" can jump from group to group, and a once great group can head downhill quickly. As I mentioned earlier, if you're a serious poster and active in Sasquatch Facebook groups, you may be invited to join secret groups. These groups are secret to admit only like-minded people. I've joined a few, and left a few.

Speaking of leaving groups, I leave any group whose members accuse others of lying and hoaxing. There is no way for one member to know if another is hoaxing something unless you know that person well. Most scoffers are either trolls or simply disagree with what is posted. One can't learn anything from those people, so to me, I feel it better to simply move on.

But one thing I think all groups are useful for is sharing information. Interest in Sasquatch is at an all time high, with the many types of groups allowing the explosion of those with an interest in all things Sasquatch.

Many are secretive about their Sasquatch research. Why, I'm not sure. But I think most serious researchers are very open about what they know, and many even write books about it.

Chapter 33: Another Hand Print

Monday, May 18, 2015. This is almost getting old. We now check our car daily for prints, and this morning we found another. Three actually. They are all of the left hand. The first was on the silver part of the car and so very hard to photograph. The next two were on the window and very plain. Odd, no thumb print. Only part of the palm and some finger tips. Small too. The hand was cupped so there is no way to tell how big the hand was, but the print measured six and a half inches from palm base to finger tip.

We're thinking that this is a small juvenile because of the small hand prints and the small trees that were broken and twisted at our cabin. It might be coming around because it can smell both dog and horse in the car since the dogs ride back there and there was some horse thing stashed there for a time, like a horse blanket and saddle. It might be curious about the scent.

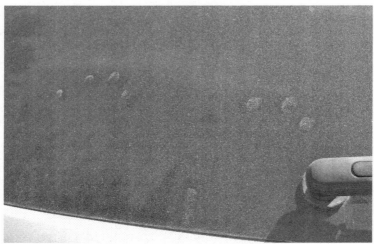

Tonight we're thinking of leaving the back hatch open and maybe putting a banana or something back there to see what we get.

Chapter 34: Odd Happenings

I'm starting to think that our local Sasquatch is a juvenile, based on the hand prints we recently found, and it is messing with us. Kind of like how when we were kids and we'd ring doorbells and run away.

Wednesday, May 20, 2015. I'll admit it. I've lost it. It is a good thing I'm old because otherwise I would never admit to doing some of the things I do.

We've had what I suspect is a juvenile Sasquatch coming around the cabin every night, and sometimes in the day.

Yesterday morning, I went to our property to stake the goats out before running errands off the mountain. I got beer and went down the hill to check on the goats, and laying there in plain view was a bright blue bungee cord. It was not there at 10 AM. I certainly would have seen it. Did a Sasquatch trade a bar of soap for a bungee cord? Can I even write that without risk of being committed?

Pam arrived at the property from work early in the afternoon, and late in the day we left for the cabin. She arrived minutes before me. As I drove down the driveway, I saw the door to the wood shed was open and Pam was walking about inspecting the ground.

"What are you looking for?" I asked.

"Foot prints."

"Why did you open the wood shed door?"

"I didn't", she said.

Huh. It must be the juvenile Sasquatch.

I read someplace that Sasquatch like apples, bananas, and other fruit. Me being me, I put a banana on the roof of the car last night. This morning, I went out to check it first thing. This is what I found.

We had some rain last night. The finger prints left yesterday are almost gone, as you can see if you look closely to the left of the wiper. But if you look just above the wiper, you will see a single finger print. There is no road dust because of the rain. It was dusted during the night with pollen.

It is as if the Sasquatch said "OK, I was here and I found that yellow thing. Exactly what is it and what do I do with it?"

In the future, we shall leave only food that a local Sasquatch would know.

Chapter 35: The Professionals Come in

Once you're interested in Sasquatch, you'll be joining Facebook groups about them. You'll also soon receive friend requests from people you do not know from these groups. I accept all of them. No, I am not worried about weirdos and cyber-stalkers. I've been playing on Al Gores' internets since the very beginning and I have yet to come across any serious threats.

Such was the case in May when I received a friend request from Ted. As I usually do, I checked his profile to make sure he was somewhat normal, and he was, so I accepted it. Shortly thereafter, I received a Facebook message from Ted. He asked if I had talked to Steve Kulls, a noted Sasquatch researcher who also happens to live in the area. Steve has been on a number of television shows regarding Sasquatch and is knowledgeable on the subject.

We made arrangements to meet on our property and not the cabin, since the cabin is impossible to find, on Thursday, June 3rd, 2015. They arrived late, around 7 PM, being held up by rush hour traffic. Ted and Steve both seemed like pleasant folk, common sense and down to earth. Pam and I showed them a tree branch twist, and then the "nest", which Steve took a special interest in. He measured the opening (two feet) and then stuck his head inside.

"Its bigger in here than you think," he said.

He was particularly interested in the fact that our dogs won't go in there. Not even Olivia, our German Shorthaired Pointer, who crawls into anything in search of mice.

We remarked that we've had absolutely no activity on our property this year and didn't know why. But as we were looking for a territory marker that we found last year, we found out why.

Just over our property line, on state land, was a game camera. That explained it. Put up a trail cam and Sasquatches vanish. Some think they can detect infrared, others think that Sasquatches simply know when something is out of place or added to their forest.

We then had Ted and Steve follow us to the cabin. There, we showed them the small tree breaks and twists by the cabin door, various tree bends and structures, where the car was parked when we found the hand prints, the well where Pam found the first foot print, and a general tour of the place. Ted and Steve didn't say much.

"Well, do you think we might have Sasquatches here?" asked Pam.

Steve paused for a moment, and then said "You could have an HBO special here."

Before they left, Steve showed us some of his gear. He has a digital night vision viewer, a directional heat sensor, and explained about his eight camera DVR setup. They do not generally whoop and holler in the woods, and certainly would never harm a Sasquatch if they saw one.

A few days later, Ted messaged me on Facebook again, asking if he could bring a team to the cabin to spend a night. Pam and I talked about it and agreed but only on the condition that all team members would not divulge our last names or location. We want to make sure that whomever comes here is serious about studying and researching Sasquatch, not crazy, and will not give us unwanted publicity. We want to protect our Sasquatches and leave them be. They've done us no harm and we think we should reciprocate.

Chapter 36: Gone Squatchin'

The word "squatchin'" means trekking off into the field to look for signs of Sasquatch. For the first time, Pam and I, and our friend Bill, decided to hike up the mountain from our cabin to where we think the Sasquatches are headed to look for signs of them. Did we find any? Maybe. We think so. Yes.

We first followed the creek that runs by the cabin, and we found all kinds of tree bends and tree structures. But the problem with those is trying to determine if they could have simply fallen or bent that way by natural means, or needed to be placed that way by some intelligent being.

It is thought that Sasquatch may mark trails by bending over or breaking saplings and pinning the ends down with sticks and logs. In a forest with hundreds of vertical trees, a bent sapling stands out.

Especially when it is hard to imagine that nature pinned the end down. This requires careful inspection and an objective mind.

Perhaps the most exciting for me was finding a huge footprint in the leafy forest floor, fully eighteen inches long. I know it is hard to see in this photo below, but the heel is to the left, and the toes are to the right.

Giant poop. Sasquatch or bear. We found lots of it. Sorry to be graphic, but the diameter of this scat indicates either a huge bear or a Sasquatch.

Me, looking exhausted from the climb.

But the view from the top was spectacular. It is easy to see how a large Sasquatch could stay undetected.

This is a good example of a tree bend made by something other than nature. The tree on the right is bent over and pinning the tree from the left, but the tree on the right is itself pinned by a log.

Yet another tree bend.

While I think we found evidence of Sasquatch, it doesn't mean much of anything to me. Why? Pam and I already know that Sasquatch exist and are around us. Finding more evidence doesn't add anything to our beliefs.

But it is still fun to find, and 'squatching is simply hiking with a purpose. But it was a beautiful day to go for a hike in the woods, and there were no bugs. A wonderful day.

Chapter 37: Another Print

July 6, 2015. Yet another print on the back of the Kia. I don't know what it is about our car, but Sasquatches seem to love the back window.

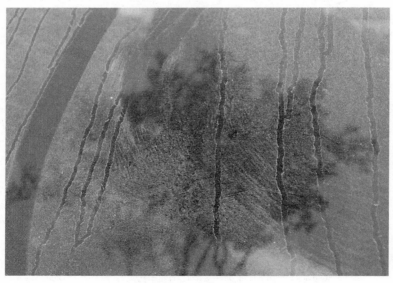

I certainly can't say it was a Sasquatch, but it was some animal with long fur or hair that stands at least six feet tall. As you can see in the close-up photo, it had long fur.

Pam went squatchin' a few days ago and found an old tree stump by the cabin that had a pine bough stuck in it. Thinking that it might be some kind of a signature, she added some ferns to it. She checked a couple of days later and the ferns were removed and tossed on the ground. She put them back.

A couple of nights ago, we were sitting in our cabin, Pam on her iPad and me on my laptop, at 10:30 at night. There was a loud banging on the east wall of the cabin. Apparently, the Sasquatch was letting us know that Pam was not to add ferns to his stump.

A few days later, Pam checked the stump and found pine cone scales on it. This wouldn't normally be interesting except there are no cone bearing pine trees nearby, and taken in context with everything else she's found, she decided to look closer. She found many more pine cone scales on the hill close to the cabin, and the ground was tramped down, as if a Sasquatch spent a lot of time standing there, eating pine cones and watching us.

And then, returning to our cabin after a day on our property, we found a stem of a day lily with three buds on it placed in the vestibule, inside the outer screen door. I don't know how it could have gotten there unless something or someone placed it there. It is interesting to think that perhaps our juvenile Sasquatch gave us a present. Or more likely, gave Pam a present.

It seemed to be taking a liking to her.

Chapter 38. The Washers

OK, so this is weird. Not that everything so far isn't, but this borders on insane (file under "C"). And a stretch of the imagination. I went to our property to let our dogs run and to let the goats out of the horse trailer, as I do every day. There, on the steps of the tractor-trailer trailer that we use for storage, were a handful of washers, a hose clamp, and an odd looking barrel nut. What the heck? Where did these come from?

I mentioned it to Pam, and she said that the goats had been in the tractor-trailer trailer the day before and they probably knocked them out and onto the steps. Nope. I keep all of my nuts and bolts and washers in an antique pretzel can that belonged to my dad, and that was still intact with the lid still on. That wasn't it. Where did they come from?

Many believe that Sasquatches are highly evolved apes. Very smart, and also very curious and playful. I posted a photo of the "gift" on a Facebook Sasquatch page, and a person quickly came back and noticed that everything left was round. The washers, the hose clamp, and the barrel nut. Hmmmm....

That got me thinking. I had left a golf ball sitting on a beer can along the game trail, thinking that a Sasquatch might find it interesting and take it. One did not. But perhaps the Sasquatch thought I was fascinated by round things, and so brought me more as a gift.

One has to be careful when "gifting" animals, including Sasquatches. You certainly don't want to make one expect things and then not get it. But Pam left four blackberries on her "gifting stump". The next day, one was bitten in half. The others were left. Nope, no idea what that means, other than maybe an acknowledgment of thanks for the berries.

But round metal things? Where did it find them? Along the road? Our neighbor's hunting camp? Why give them to me? To let me know it is about and watching me? To let me know that it accepts me?

I'm starting to think that Sasquatches are not simply an ape.

Chapter 39: Sasquatch Chatter

July 24, 2015. Pam woke me up at 4 AM this morning, saying there was a bunch of Sasquatches outside the cabin. I awoke groggily and heard... something. I also hadn't conceded that I needed hearing aids yet and low noises evaded me. So me being me, I took action. I rolled back over and went back to sleep.

What Pam said she heard were whoops and monkey chatter of at least four Sasquatches. She didn't mean that the Sasquatches were monkeys, of course, but that the vocalizations were a rapid staccato. She could hear them move the brush as they passed by the cabin. Olivia, the German Shorthaired Pointer, was going ballistic. The pit bulls, being very intelligent dogs, were hiding, as they do when Sasquatches are about.

These Sasquatches were traveling up the trail on the north side of the cabin, opposite of where our local guy hangs out. Maybe they avoid each other? Who knows, but there are two trails for some reason. Maybe one is an HOV lane for two or more Sasquatches. Or more likely, our side is the rest area.

Chapter 40; Sasquatch Poop?

I've been disappointed this year. We still have a lot of Sasquatch activity at our rental cabin, but nothing on our own property that we're building on a mile down the road. That's changed as of today.

It was a rainy day here and I wasn't going to get any building done, so Pam and I took a trip to the Iroquois Indian Museum at Howe's Cave, NY. It was a delightful place and we both enjoyed it. As we were leaving and Pam was buying a necklace, I took the opportunity to ask the man if he had heard any stories of Sasquatch and the Iroquois. He smiled slyly and didn't say much, other than that he had heard some stories as a boy. But next to him, the woman's face lit up, and Pam and she had a very animated conversation about Sasquatch. She said that the Iroquois refer to them as the Keepers of the Forest and watch over everything that happens.

When we got home, we grabbed our dogs and headed to our property. The pointer usually dashes off through the woods, but would not today. She and the two pit bulls just kept barking at something, but wouldn't go into the woods. That means one thing. Sasquatch. Heck, our dogs chase after black bears.

Pam went to investigate and returned to say that the Sasquatch have a new trail just along the wood line, and have what she called "watching stations", places where they stand and watch us. Later, she found what is in these photos.

Pam has found many foot prints, and it seems that there is at least one adult and one very small juvenile, maybe a toddler. In the first photo (I know it is hard to see in the book) is a foot print.

The second is a very small bed, perhaps where a toddler Sasquatch took a nap and played with a stick, and also pooped the bed.

The third is poop (sorry).

The fourth is a close-up of the poop, which has both fur and a small branch, so it isn't a carnivore, it is an omnivore.

We're both happy our Sasquatches are back.

Chapter 41: The Professionals Step Back In

August 7, 2015: Awhile back, two professionals, Steve and Ted, came here from Albany to look around. Ted belongs to a Facebook Sasquatch group that I also belong to, and me being me and being very open, I often post things that Pam and I find. Ted messaged me and asked if he and Steve Kulls could come to look around. They did and were interested in what they saw. They came back last night, arriving a little after 8 PM. They donned all their gear, and they and Pam spent a few hours "squatching". I did not. I'm not observant to begin with, hard of hearing, and night blind. There would be no point.

I went to bed around 10. At 11, I was awakened by either Ted or Steve "whooping", which is making a very loud ape-like vocalization. And then I heard it. An answering whoop. And then another. And then another. Our three dogs starting barking, and then (so I was told because I couldn't hear due to all of the commotion in the cabin) the coyotes started howling.

The three hiked up to the top of our driveway. Steve was looking around with his heat-sensing equipment and saw something very large by our landing on the highway. Bear? It stood up and ran off. Steve would only say that it was very large.

They came back down the driveway to where their car was parked. They were discussing what they'd heard and seen when something knocked on our Kia to get their attention. It worked. They investigated and saw nothing, but Ted duplicated the sound by whacking the hood of the car.

Steve and Ted were very impressed and pleased with what they'd seen and heard. Steve has two hours of recordings. They want to come back with a full investigative team to our property. They'll camp there and spend the whole night. I'll stay home with the dogs.

Chapter 42: The Horse's Mane

This is interesting.

Pam and I spend summers in the southern Adirondacks of upstate New York. We've been finding Sasquatch evidence since we learned about them a year ago.

This year, they've been leaving us things. First, it was a bright blue bungee cord. Then it was a bunch of large washers, a locking pin off a tractor, and a hose clamp (all round items).

Pam and I just spent five days camping out there. On the third day, we found this on the ground by Pam's car. It is from a horse's mane on the property next door to us. Part of the mane was wound up around it to tie it into a bow.

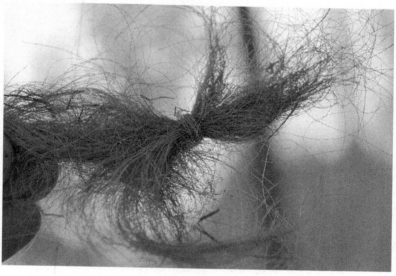

No, it is not anyone playing tricks on us. First, our 38,000 acre town only has 550 residents. We have one neighbor, my 83 year old father-in-law who thinks the whole subject of Sasquatch is silly. Besides, this was left at night, and he's in bed by 8.

At the cabin that we rent a mile away, we get a lot of Sasquatch activity, and they seem to really like Pam. She found a stump outside the window wall of our cabin where they seem to watch us, since the ground is all tramped down around it. Pam left them an earring recently, which they ignored. Just before we left to go camping, she cut an apple in half and left it on the stump. When we returned to the cabin tonight, the earring and half the apple were on the half of the stump towards the cabin. The other half of the apple was gone. I've read that they share.

Fascinating. Sasquatch merely an ape? I don't think so.

Chapter 43: The Smell!

August 24, 2015; Olivia the dog had to go out at 3 AM last night. I admonished her not to bark. For once, she listened. For about ten minutes. Then she started barking frantically. I slipped on my sneakers, grabbed a flashlight, and went looking for her. This was going to be trouble because she only listens to Pam and ignores me.

She was halfway up our long driveway. I couldn't see her, but I could tell about where she was by her barking.

"Olivia! Come! This way!" I yelled.

Much to my surprise, her eyes shone in the light of the flashlight as she came running to me, something she never does. When she's on the scent of something, her German Shorthaired Pointer instincts take over and she's totally focused on whatever it is she's after.

"Good girl Olivi..." and then she ran at full speed right past me and into the cabin. Huh. I stood there looking around with the small LED flashlight, seeing nothing. And then I smelled it. I have a lousy sense of smell. Pam has to tell me when the garbage stinks and to take it out. But I could smell something foul. If I can smell it, it must be pungent. And it must have been close. I paddled my butt into the cabin too.

The smell is hard to describe. It was a combination of garbage, feces, and body order. It was bad.

For the first time since we've been here, I probably smelled a Sasquatch. This has been reported by others, but most accounts say they've smelled nothing. I guess I should feel special, or honored or something.

Chapter 44: The Gifting Stump

I've gotten to the point in my Sasquatch experience that, when I see a tree bend or twist, or if Pam shows me a pic of a foot print, I simply shrug my shoulders. It is like finding a beer can on the side of the road and exclaiming "Look honey! A litter bug was here!". But what I find fascinating is Pam's interactions with our Sasquatch.

This has been going on for a few weeks and so there is no date to attach to it.

Steve Kulls, a well known researcher who was here awhile back, looked at the window wall on our cabin, towards the nearby wood line, and told us we had Sasquatch TV here. He said he wouldn't be surprised at all if they stood along the wood line at night to watch us.

Pamela, being Pamela, started looking around out there. She found an old tree stump, and the ground around it was tramped down. On it were pine nuts. Maybe just squirrels? Or maybe a Sasquatch standing there, watching us, and munching on snacks. Stuck into the stump was a pine bough. Pam decided to add some ferns to it.

The next day, the ferns were cast aside. On the stump were three sticks roughly arranged into something that resembled the lettter A. Pam added a stick to make a P. The next day, it was still there.

Pam left a dragonfly earring, having lost the other one. That too was untouched.

Then she cut an apple in half and left both halves on the stump. The next day, one half was gone and the other placed on Pam's side of the stump with her earring placed on top.

This morning (September 1st), Pamela checked the stump. There were a number of berries on the ground around the stump, like they were dropped. They weren't berries that grow around the cabin. They were something like an elderberry, we're not sure. But they didn't come from here. Pam picked them up and placed them on the stump. Tonight, they were still there, but each one was carefully smooshed with a finger.

Last night (still September 1st) Pam and I were outside taking star photos and while doing so, Pam heard clucking noises, like a roosting chicken would make. She assumed it must be a grouse. Later, she and I were sitting at our dining table. There was a light tapping on the corner window of our window wall. Sassy the cat was still out and Pam called for her, but she didn't come. Then there was a scraping noise on the cabin wall. I looked out the small kitchen window and saw nothing. This morning, Pam found marks on the corner window that look like they were made by fingers, about six feet above the ground.

In the sand next to the corner window, she found a large foot print in the sand, and farther back from the cabin another.

Today, September 2nd, we found a half a squirrel by Pam's car. The back half. The tail was completely flattened to the point that it looked like a bird feather. There was a hole where it's innards used to be. Part of it's spine was missing. It was pulled apart with great force, it seems. I wrote before that Sasquatch share from many reports I've read. Maybe in repayment for the apple, the Sasquatch left Pam half a squirrel.

Our Sasquatch seem to like Pam and are willing to interact with her. I'm still unsure what they think about me.

Chapter 45: Eye Shine and Lights

First, let me start off that I am NOT saying that the following is Sasquatch. I think it is a strange atmospheric phenomenon following a Sasquatch visit. Coincidence. Probably. Who knows.

September 4, 2015; Pam and I got home late yesterday, about 9:30 PM (late for us). Pam left lights on in the cabin because she knew we'd be getting home after dark. We got out of our car and walked towards the cabin door, and Pam froze and stopped me (I'm night blind and she has to lead me around).

"David! There's something big rustling in those bushes!" as she was pointing to the wood line by the cabin. I didn't hear a thing because I'm also hard of hearing.

Then I saw it for the first time. Red eye shine, reflected by the lights on in the cabin. I only saw one eye, and it was a bright red color.

In the cabin, Pam said the stars were very bright, so I went back outside to take star photos. Each was five seconds in duration. They were all normal, except this one.

I know the photo above won't print well in this book, but I'm including it anyway. Don't worry, cropped images from the above photo are coming up.

No, I have no idea what it is. I do NOT believe that Sasquatch turn into orbs of light and fly off in UFOs, but the coincidence here was startling, and amusing. To me anyway.

Here are two photos cropped from the one above.

Nope. No idea.

It looks like a meandering ball of light, electrical in nature. The skies were clear with no thunderstorms or any other electrical activity in the area.

There was nothing in the photo before this, or after this. The lights were there for no more than thirty seconds because that is the length of the exposure.

I guess this fits the description of a UFO, but of course, it is not an alien spaceship. Unless the aliens were drinking, which I suppose is possible.

Chapter 46: Infrasound

Tonight, I was sitting home alone, Pam off horseback riding. Suddenly, the cabin started to shake and I could barely hear a very, very low noise of some sort. I called my friend Bill who lives about five miles from here. His house didn't shake, so no earthquake. Infrasound maybe? At this point, knowing we have Sasquatches about and understanding what they're capable of, I'm open to anything.

Infrasound is low frequency sound that is lower than a human's ability to hear, below 20 Hz. For a person to detect infrasound, the sound generated must be felt. Many animals are capable of infrasound and use it to either stun prey or to communicate. These include whales, elephants, alligators, hippopotamus, rhinocerous, and giraffes. And Sasquatch, many think.

Elephants use infrasound to communicate over very long distances of 7 miles or more. Could our Sasquatch do the same? Or, as is thought of some predators, infrasound is used to stun prey to make it easier to catch.

Chapter 47; the Steak

Yesterday, September 6th, I was putting things in the backseat of my car to leave our property that we're building on and to head to the cabin we rent for the night. There in the back seat was boxed leftovers from the night before. I wasn't going to eat it, so I opened the container and placed it on top of our grill, putting it about five feet off the ground.

Today, I arrived at the property. The container was right where I left it on the grill, but the steak was gone. Whatever got it could reach up at least five feet, ruling out every area creature except one. Something tall and dexterous that could pluck a steak out of a styrofoam container without knocking it off the grill.

Chapter 48; Sasquatch Easter Eggs

Our friendly neighborhood Sasquatch has been leaving us things. At our rental cabin, it leaves Pam gifts of food, like a mighty fine back half of a squirrel bitten cleanly in two and with the guts and spine removed for her convenience. On our property, it has left me two bungee cords and an assortment of washers, three point hitch locking pin, barrel nut, and a hose clamp (all round things).

Pam is incredibly observant. She was checking the game trail that both deer and Sasquatch use, and called me down.

The first pic is from standing on the game trail and looking towards the woods. The area in question is in shadows, on the right.

This photo is of the log that our Sasquatch may be sitting on to watch us. What log? Exactly.

The photo above is a log (from which it can sit and watch us clearly) with an "A" stick structure behind it, which we see frequently.

The photo above? A fuel filter. Yep. That's right. It smelled of diesel, and would have come from a John Deere, White, or Allis Chalmers tractor. I have a gas powered 1952 Ferguson TO-30 so it isn't mine.

I've decided to start referring to things Sasquatch left for us to find, things not in plain sight, as "Easter Eggs".

Chapter 49: Sasquatch Intelligence

We found our first foot print in August of 2014. As you now know, I have a tendency to research things to death. It is what I do. Anything I feel I need to know, I study in depth. The subject of Sasquatch was no different. I devoured multiple books, googled it intensely, and joined groups on Facebook. There is something that I haven't found an answer to. How intelligent are Sasquatch?

Most academics, like professor Meldrum, consider Sasquatch to be a North American ape. Native Americans consider them to be just another tribe of people. From Pam's and my experiences, they are capable of reason, and share things, and are very intelligent.

This brings to mind our time living on our trawler and traveling down the eastern seaboard. We were often joined by dolphin who would frolic in our bow wave, and as we excitedly looked at them, they'd roll on their sides to watch us watching them. Since intelligence is measured by the number of folds in a brain, they are thought to be more intelligent than humans, which must be so since they don't work and pay taxes. They swim, eat and play all day, and have sex just for fun.

Could the same be said of Sasquatch? They don't work and pay taxes either, and live off the land.

My opinion of Sasquatch is evolving, quickly. I don't think they're an ape, like a Mountain Gorilla, but more like people. Pam heard a group pass by the cabin one night not long ago. What woke her up was that they were talking to each other in a sort of monkey chatter. People talk to each other, dolphins talk to each other, so why not Sasquatch?

Chapter 50: The Real Wayne's World

On September 20th, 2015 Pam and I, Pam's mom Judi, and our friend Bill were doing our usual Friday night thing at Vrooman's restaurant in Caroga Lake for wings. We were sitting at the bar and I was sitting next to a fella dressed in motorcycle gear. We struck up a conversation. Wayne is a free spirit, He lived on a sailboat for a time, sold it, and bought a motorcycle to cruise around in He was traveling from Michigan to Maine before heading to Pennsylvania to work on a farm and then on to Florida.

Wayne was tenting at night. I offered him the use of our RV which he gratefully accepted. We dropped him off and warned him about our Sasquatches. They won't bother you, we told him, but be aware that they're here.

I think you'll enjoy his video. We come in at the 8:30 mark.

Type this into your browser and be prepared to laugh...

https://www.youtube.com/watch?v=OUA__WZjGfA or search for

"Exploring and old Amusement Park,Motorcycle Diaries episode 5 Adirondacks/The real wayne world" on You Tube.

Chapter 51: Pamela's Sasquatch Friend

Pamela and I have been busy lately. Friday was a reunion with childhood friends, Saturday was a wedding, and Sunday Pam worked most of the day, and then it was to her mom's house for dinner. Pam's Sasquatch friend must have missed her walking the trails by the cabin. At 12:30 AM, there was an unmistakable knock on the cabin. Pam's friend was back and looking for her.

This morning, Tuesday, September 15th, 2015, Pam arose for work. But first, she checked the stump. Yep. There it was. The dead leaf was removed from the stump shard, and a fresh leaf replaced it. On the leaf was a moth, freshly deceased. It sort of resembled the dragon fly earring that Pam left on the stump long ago, and the leaf seems to symbolize Pamela, perhaps because of her ponytail.

The moth was quite dead. I poked it. Imagine the gentleness and dexterity it took for a large Sasquatch to do this. And the gentleness and sensitivity of spirit, and kindness and fondness it has for Pam.

Chapter 52: More From the Gifting Stump

September 23rd, 2015. Pam's latest Sasquatch "gifting stump" encounter... I hate using the term gifting stump, but I honestly don't know what else to call it.

It doesn't look like much, but Pam's half is on the far side of the stump, and Sas's is closest. Pam's forest friend (I assume. What else?) moved her dragonfly earring from her side to his side.

I wish I could figure out what things like this mean.

Only one more month and all this ends as we head to Florida. We won't be returning to this cabin in the Spring, but will be on our own property a mile down the road, staying in our RV as we start building our little house. We also have Sasquatch activity there, and a lot of it, but Pam really wants her Sasquatch friend to find her there.

Chapter 53: Searching For Sasquatch

I've never been into Finding Bigfoot kind of TV shows, even when I had TV, which was years ago. It all seemed quite silly to me. But a local guy with some reknown, Steve Kulls of Sasquatch Detective, took an interest in our Sasquatch activity.

Steve and his partner Ted made a couple of trips from the Albany area to our place to scope it out. They saw the tree twists and such, and came back to spend a few hours one night not long ago. Before leaving, Steve asked Pam if he could whoop. Pam said yes and Steve did. He got three responses.

September 27, 2015; Steve and his full research team arrived at our property to set up camp and do some serious research. Pam and I were taken aback by the number of people arriving.

There had to be at least a dozen people, many of them heavily armed.

I stayed at the cabin and dog-sat, and Pam joined the team. They were pretty much skunked that night, as often happens when searching for Sasquatch. You don't find them, they find you, they say. But Steve said he detected movement around the camp, and Pam reported, for the first time, rocks being tossed in her direction, enough to make her jump. Rock tossing is thought to be a warning. Stay away! Far enough!

The next morning, by ten AM, everyone was gone. I know they froze their butts off, but I hope they at least enjoyed camping out and that everyone had a good time.

We don't find stuff everyday either. Better luck next time.

Chapter 54: Humm...

September 28, 2015; OK... this is going to border on the weird. OK OK, weirder. For that, I apologize in advance.

I love sitting on our property. It doesn't matter what the weather is. I dress for it and enjoy nature and that all around me.

Two days ago, I was at our land. It was a cold, rainy, miserable day, but I bundled up and drove from our rental cabin to our place a mile down the road from the cabin after loading up our three dogs. Upon arrival, they gleefully escaped from the car and scampered off. I went to the run-in shed and let Amos and Andy, our two goats, out to graze.

I sat in our screen house in the rain, reading "Visits from the Forest People" about the experiences of folks in Oregon with things happening very similar to Pam's and mine. I love sitting on our property. I hear birds, and many forest critters whose calls I cannot identify, me being a city boy and all. But then I heard a hum. It was a hummmm... hummmm.... hummmm... hummm...

What the heck? I listened for some kind of truck or machinery traveling down our road, but nothing passed by. Hummmm.... hummmm... hummm....

No idea.

And then I read in my book that these folk experienced many sounds from their Oregon Sasquatch, including a hum. It kind of freaked me out.

And then it all stopped. I haven't heard it since.

Chapter 55: Signature Markers

Pam and I actually have no idea what these are and what they mean, but we've been referring to them as signature markers. They come in different formats and we think they may be signatures from different Sasquatches, sort of like calling cards. Pam found this right outside our cabin's window yesterday afternoon, October 5, 2015.

Our friendly neighborhood Sasquatch always makes his sign in the rough letter "A" shape. Pam first found it on the gifting stump months ago, and many times since then.

She designed a dragonfly signature herself and left it on the stump a couple of days ago, and her Sasquatch answered her.

Yes, she also left it a few puffballs which it apparently doesn't care for, but above that is her signature marker. It looks like an airplane to me.

October 9, 2015. I decided to do some google investigation on Al Gore's internets, and searched for a symbol that resembled the letter "A". Since Sasquatch are thought to possibly be Asian in ancestry, I started there. I quickly found it. It is "dai" or "dae". It is the same in Mandarin, Catonese, Hakka, Min Nan, and Wu. It is the same in Japanese, Korean, Vietnamese, and Mulam. It means "big man". What I still don't know is whether it is referring to Pam and me, or it.

October 10, 2015. Pam went out to check her Sasquatch stump tonight and came running back into the cabin very excited.

"David come quick!"

"Should I bring my camera?"

"YES!!"

Pam's dragonfly was rearranged into the familiar letter "A" shape. I noticed a small stick laying on the left leg of the A.

162

An inverted V means "man" in Chinese.

A horizontal line across it means"big".

The small twig on the left leg of the A shape means "great".

Hmmm.... Great. Big. Man.

October 14, 2015. *(This is from Pamela.)*

Who can spot the differences? I left the stump where my Sasquatch shares things with me..... my "dragonfly" mark on the right, my own "A" made from two red leaf stems and a small stick on the left, my dragonfly earring lying next to the "A" lying face up and flat and a cattail across the center of the stump. This morning it was all rearranged. Hmmm. *smile emoticon here* I like playing stump chess with my hairy friend. I just wish I could figure out what the "A" symbol means to them. *(at this point, Pamela totally dismissed my nutty Chinese theory - Dave)*

164

Chapter 56: Footprint

October 14th, 2015. Footprints are the most found bit of Sasquatch evidence, but not here. The ground is too rocky and full of leaf clutter, but it is great when Pam finds one, like this one found right next to the Sasquatch stump.

Pam's foot's heel is at the Sasquatch heel. Her toe is at the mid-tarsal break (a joint large apes have that we don't). The toes are at the edge of the leaves and the corner of the photo.

Chapter 57: Whoops

Saturday, October 18th, was opening day for deer season, black powder. I arrived at our property without our dogs who were confined to the cabin. It was about noon. Within a few minutes, I heard a distant "whoooop" from up the mountain. I had never heard a whoop here before. It sounded very ape-like. Within a few minutes, there was another, and another. Every few minutes, I would hear a whoop, always coming from a different direction. It was either a moving Sasquatch, or several signaling to each other. It all stopped in about a half an hour.

I was cutting lumber when I heard someone behind me. It was my neighbor Rick, dressed in camouflage and carrying a black powder rifle. We exchanged a few pleasantries. I asked if he had any luck. Nope. He was hunting up the mountain with some buddies. I didn't ask him if he heard the whoops. I'm sure he did, and if he was open to the existence of Sasquatches, he would have told me.

Rick's friends were down the mountain, waiting for Rick to push deer their way, and off he went.

Chapter 58: Stench in the Morning

October 21st, 2015; Now that I'm retired, I tend to sleep in. When I ran my own business, I'd often go to work anywhere from 3 AM to 6 AM. Sixty hour work weeks were the norm. Now that I'm retired, 9 AM is my preferred wake time, and my work weeks (building outbuildings on our land) is about 20 hours a week.

This morning I was awakened at 6 AM by a powerful stench. Although it is fall, we still have our bedroom window open. Our bedroom is on the second floor and since heat rises, it tends to be warm up there. Anyway, the stink was so strong that it awoke me. I looked around for a farting dog but there wasn't one, and besides, this was much worse. If you own a dog, you understand how bad it was. I listened and didn't hear anything. I dozed back off, but I was awakened several more times in the next hour by the rank odor.

At 7, I grumpily arose. I told Pam about the odor. She was downstairs where the windows were closed and didn't smell it, but she said she let Olivia the Pointer out this morning and she ran around the cabin but wouldn't enter the woods like she usually does.

Sasquatch.

Chapter 59: Sasquatch and the Neighbors

Also October 21st; Our friend Bill had called us on Sunday to tell us a stray dog was under a carriage in his shed. Pam and Ruby the Pit Bull piled in the car and drove over. Before they left, I warned "Don't come home with another dog!". Sometimes a man just has to put his foot down. This is my kingdom and I am the king.

So a bit later, Pamela enters the cabin with a small female pit bull. We proceeded to try to find its owner. We posted it on Facebook and talked to our friends. Our dog control officer said a fella a named Dan lost a small female pit bull, but we couldn't find him. Our friend Bill said a neighbor around the corner was named Dan and we should see him. Plus, he and his wife have also had many Sasquatch sightings.

Really? And I'm just hearing about this now?

So we went there tonight with Lilly in hand. Becky answered the door. No, they don't have a lost dog, but then Pam asked "What about Sasquatch?"

Becky's eyes got big and her jaw dropped. "Why do you ask?"

"Because you're not crazy," said Pam. "We've seen it too."

And therein Pam, Becky, and I got into a discussion of our local Sasquatch. They've been seeing them for fourteen years here.

Becky seemed very relieved to know that we confirmed her and her husband's sightings.

Chapter 60: Chinese Symbols Continued

Over the past few weeks, I've been tinkering around with comparing our Sasquatch glyphs to Chinese symbols. So far, we've identified "big man", "great big man", "friend", and "leave" or "depart" (submitted to me by a friend).

I think the most intriguing is the symbol for "friend". It is a bit complicated and surely nothing that would fall that way in nature.

Pam was starting to buy into my nutty Chinese symbol theory a bit and asked me to look it up and draw it for her, which I did. It looks like this – 友 Sort of a lower case F with an X under the lower horizontal line.

Pam arranged sticks on the stump. The next day, she was excited. The Sasquatch did not rearrange her sticks, but removed the thick sticks that made the X and replaced them with skinny ones.

I guess Sasquatches are stickers for accuracy and proper spelling.

Chapter 61: The End

October 28, 2015. We winterized the cabin for the last time. We're not renting it again in order to focus on building our house. We'll live uncomfortably in our RV as an incentive to get a cabin built.

We loaded up our four dogs, two cats, the horse, and two goats and headed south for Florida.

Next year, Pam and I are sincerely hoping to get some Sasquatch activity on our own property a mile down the road. We know they're there, but it is not on "the Sasquatch Highway" up the mountain.

Maybe that's a good thing, not having so many Sasquatches about.. It will give me something else to obsess about. Which I do. Obsess. And over-think things, and research anything that interests me to death.

I hope you enjoyed reading of our experiences. No one is more amazed than I am. Sasquatch. Who'da thunk it. I'm so amazed, I should write a book about it.

Made in the USA
Middletown, DE
11 October 2016